HEAVENLY DREAMS

AS HE WALKS WITH ME SERIES
BOOK 1

CARLIS STUBER

Dr Jeff,

Thank you for taking
such good care of my
families Chiropractic needs.

God Bless

Darli Stober

1 Tim 4:14

Book 23

TABLE OF CONTENTS

DEDICATION

This book is first, and foremost, dedicated to my wife Faye for her diligence, patience, inspiration, guidance, and endurance as I completed this manuscript. I spent many hours in my office to complete this work.

Thank you for seeing it through with me.

I am also dedicating this book to my children Angela Leitz and Jeremy Stuber. Your inspiration and guidance have helped make this possible. I never shared much of this part of my life with you. Please forgive me for that. I have always sought God for direction regarding this information entrusted to me. Now I know what to do with it, and this work is the result. Keep the faith, staying on the straight and narrow path, like your Mom and I raised you. Continue raising your children in the same manner, always seeking God for their direction.

I also dedicate this book to all who receive inspiration from its content. My prayer is that each of you will gain some insight into your life through the dreams and visions God has given me.

ACKNOWLEDGMENTS

A special thank you to my wife Faye, my two sisters, Sharry Larson, and Diane Ashwell, and my granddaughter Krystina Stuber for their many hours of encouragement and reading as they proofread this book.

You have all been an endless source of inspiration and have served me well in your work.

I mostly want to thank our Lord and Savior Jesus Christ, who through the Holy Spirit provided the words and images included in this book. Years of His speaking to me have provided the stories through nighttime dreams. May they never cease, may I always understand their meaning, and may I always be faithful to the calling.

INTRODUCTION

This book is a journal of many of my dreams. Some of these dreams have proven prophetic and come true. Other dreams have not yet come true. I deliberately wrote the book differently than almost any other book you may read. There are nine chapters, with each chapter divided into separate stories. Each of these stories is a true story of a dream I have experienced. An application or meaning follows each for clarification or instruction. The stories, or dreams, in this book, can be read separately with no loss of plot, since each one is complete in itself. Please enjoy this book and read it from front to back, or pick the dreams you prefer to read and move around the text at will.

Following the chapters of the dreams is a section describing the purpose of sharing and an article about the author.

My greatest hope is that you will find encouragement as you read these stories. When God speaks to us in dreams, He always has a purpose. If you are experiencing Heaven sent dreams, then God has something to say to you or to say through you. Therefore, as God has revealed it to me, I have included the application or meaning of each dream.

> *"Jesus saith unto him, I am the way, the truth, and the life: no man cometh unto the Father, but by me"* *(John 14:6)*

> *"Jesus answered and said unto him, Verily, verily, I say unto thee, Except a man be born again, he cannot see the kingdom of God"* *(John 3:3)*

Statement of belief of the author:

My God is the one True God, The Trinity, God The Father, God The Son, and God The Holy Spirit. I believe in the inherency of scripture and the need for a savior (Jesus), without which there is no entrance into Heaven. Without a renewal of the inner spirit, through repentance and life changing experience known as being born-again, no person will enter into the Kingdom of God.

Carlis

"And it shall come to pass in the last days, saith God, I will pour out of my Spirit upon all flesh: and your sons and your daughters shall prophesy, and your young men shall see visions, and your old men shall dream dreams:" (Acts 2:17)

CHAPTER 1

DREAMS AND VISIONS

Where do they come from, and, could they be God communicating with us? In this series of books, I am relating some of my dreams, visions, and visitations God gave me, through the Holy Spirit. These experiences span nearly 60 years. Each is a true account. This book concentrates on dreams only. The next book in the series, titled Heavenly Experiences, will describe accounts of visions and visitations, as well as a continuation of dreams.

Not all dreams are God speaking to His people. A person has to know the difference between a God dream and what we might call a pizza dream. A pizza dream gets its name because it may be the result of what we experienced, ate, or drank the day before. These dreams will cover a variety of topics and are usually not interpretable. There are also dreams related to PTSD (Post Traumatic Stress Disorder). These dreams will relate back to some extreme stress in a person's life such as war experiences, loss of a job, loss of a spouse or child, or any life event causing extreme anxiety.

Our focus in this book is on God-given dreams. In a God dream, certain elements will leave an impression on your spirit. The Holy Spirit will quicken your spirit to understand the message given, and will always offer a precise interpretation. The interpretation may not happen the very moment you wake. Many years may pass before it's received. It might come through a word from another person, a life event, or the actual fulfillment of the dream or vision itself. As you await the interpretation, should it tarry, you will know it was a God dream by the continued presence of the elements of the dream resting in your spirit or mind. A level of anticipation will remain with you as you wait for the events to take place. They may not happen exactly as dreamt, but fulfillment or interpretation may occur in another way. The Holy Spirit will give you recall and anticipation towards the fulfillment of the dream.

DREAMS, VISIONS, AND INTERPRETATIONS

People often ask me if all elements, or items, shown in a dream are the same for everyone. I do not know since it is impossible to know how God deals with each person. When God deals with me, there are certain elements, or items, that refer to or represent other things:

- House—My being or who I am
- My Dad—Our Heavenly Father
- Siblings—Brothers and sisters in Christ
- Water—The Spirit of God
- Storms—Distress of some sort

- Machinery–Trials, hardships, or warnings of danger ahead
- Color Blue–A visitation from God
- Color Green – Peace

Visions, open visions, and visitations most often happen while I am awake. Visions may be inward, where the spirit senses or sees something that is not visible outwardly. Open visions are seeing things with the eyes that are happening around us. Visitations are experiences of supernatural visitors appearing to us, even if others do not see them.

I have experienced many open visions. When I was younger, it was difficult to distinguish between reality, imagination, and vision. While I still have a very vivid imagination, the difference today is, I have learned how to hear the voice of God, and I have learned how to identify when God is speaking. Hearing and understanding, however, are not without mistakes. Anyone who says they always have an interpretation or the only interpretation is operating in a spirit of pride. *"For now we see through a glass, darkly; but then face to face: now I know in part; but then shall I know even as also I am known" (1 Corinthians 13:12)*

In addition to dreams and visions, many people are experiencing God in visitations, and in what I call "knowings." "Knowings" are experiencing God speaking to us, or through us, mostly in our spirits, and we just "know" that it is God. I am no exception to this. In this series of books, I will be relating dreams, visions, and experiences with Almighty God. I print this with all humility, in the hopes that others will reach out to God and experience all that He has for them.

APPLICATION OR MEANING

Think about the many times you have had recurring dreams. Have you often asked yourself why you experience the same dream over and over? Have you had dreams that left you feeling like there was more to the dream than just a nighttime experience? Your spirit may feel excited or curious following the dream. These feelings are usually an indication that God is talking to you. Ask Him what it means and He will tell you. He is not withholding information or secrets from us. He is reaching out, all the time, getting His messages through to those who will listen. Many of the messages transmitted to us happen through dreams or visions.

CHAPTER 2

HEAVENLY VISITATIONS

"I knew a man in Christ above four-teen years ago, (whether in the body, I cannot tell; or whether out of the body, I cannot tell: God knoweth;) such an one caught up to the third heaven" (2 Corinthians 12:2)

The Apostle Paul spoke these words regarding an individual he knew. Three times in my life, I have experienced these same types of visitations. I cannot boldly state that I visited Heaven; but neither can I deny that I may have been there. Some have said to me, "If you were there, you would know it." I disagree with that statement since even Paul was unsure of at least one event like this.

In this chapter, I am going to share with you three heavenly visitations; whether in the spirit or the body, I do not know for sure. The first two visitations involved seeing Jesus and in the third visitation, I saw many buildings and parts of heaven. I was with someone whose face I did not see. It may have been Jesus, but I do not know his identity for sure.

VISITATION #1
BEING TAUGHT BY JESUS

Setting:

I was ten years old, and in the hospital having my appendix removed. I remember lying on the rolling bed, as we passed through the hallways on my way to surgery. The last thing I saw were the bright lights of the operating room. The lights seem to be the final push to put me asleep for the surgery.

I never told anyone what happened after I saw the operating room lights until I awoke in the recovery room. Only recently did I share this with my family. They encouraged me to share with others, which I admit, was another prompt to write this book.

Sequence of events:

I see the bright lights of the operating room and then I succumb to the anesthesia. I do not know anything about what was happening in the operating room, but I vividly remember what took place in my spirit. I found myself sitting on a sandy beach of a river. Intuitively, I knew it was the river Jordan, a symbolic entrance to Heaven. There were dozens of children about my age sitting around me while Jesus taught us. Sometimes He was standing in our midst and sometimes He was walking amongst us talking. Though I do not know what He was saying exactly, I do know that He was teaching us. There was no semblance of time. We were not in a hurry nor did Jesus seem to be anxious about how long the class would last. Suddenly, it felt like someone yanked me out of the class and off the sandy beach. I awoke fighting for my breath as I sat up on my recovery bed. A nurse pushed me down again onto the bed. Although I was fighting for breath, I seemed just to fall asleep as soon as she pushed me down. I awoke hours later in a hospital room where my parents were waiting for me.

Whether I was there in the body or the spirit, I do not know, but I do know that I was there, in Heaven. It is a beautiful, peaceful place. Jesus is everything we hear of Him to be. He wore white gowns and was as gentle as a lamb yet His words were so powerful each one seemed to draw a picture. His voice is so mellow and yet so loud I believe anyone could hear it, no matter what his or her location. I have never forgotten that visitation. I am confident of this; no one who sees Heaven will ever stop sharing with others, the need to make Heaven their eternal home.

APPLICATION OR MEANING

This dream was the beginning of my dreams, visions, and experiences with God. This one event was the launching platform for my life-time of experiences.

Everyone's experience will be a little different. God is a God of creativity and makes each of us unique. Therefore, each of us will have unique experiences, and yet they will have some similarity. Have you had an experience that you can look back upon and say, "That was my launching point for my life of richness with God?" Try to think of any times or experiences where you felt the presence of God so real it changed you forever. Then praise God for speaking into your life.

VISITATION #2
ACROSS THE JORDAN

Setting:

This particular Heavenly visit happened when I was nineteen years old, and was once again following surgery.

Sequence of events:

I check into the hospital and settle into my room. I receive preparation for surgery, and then wheeled into the operating room. During surgery, I again experience a heavenly visitation. I recognize that I am once again at the river Jordan, only this time I am standing on the bank looking across the river. I can see Jesus teaching children just as I had experienced in my last visitation, but this time I am unable to get to the other side. I am afraid and crying because I cannot get to Jesus. I do not know why I cannot get to Jesus. Is it because it is not my time to get there or is it because I am a sinner not forgiven. In the midst of this turmoil, I awake and find myself on a bed in the hospital with doctors and nurses standing around me. I hear one doctor say, "It may have been a blood clot passing through his lung." I immediately fall back to sleep.

Later, I wake and feel the horror and emptiness of that separation from Jesus, which I experienced at the Jordan River. I commit myself right then and there to learn more of what was required to cross over the river and to spend eternity with Jesus.

APPLICATION OR MEANING

The Apostle John writes, *"These things have I written unto you that believe on the name of the Son of God; that ye may know that ye have eternal life, and that ye may believe on the name of the Son of God" (John 5:13)*

God wants us to know for sure we are saved and going to heaven. He will use any means possible to get us there. This visitation taught me two things: 1) it was not my time to go to heaven and 2) how it felt to see Jesus, but not be able to get to Him. It takes repentance and obedience to get to spend eternity with Jesus. It is my prayer if you have not yet done so, that you will repent of your sin and make Jesus the Lord of your life.

VISITATION #3
HEAVENS BUILDINGS

The Apostle Paul recorded this about an individual. *"I knew a man in Christ above fourteen years ago, (whether in the body, I cannot tell; or whether out of the body, I cannot tell: God knoweth;) such an one caught up to the third heaven" (2 Corinthians 12:2)*

Having visited Heaven two times in the past, I recognize this as a visitation more than a dream. However, I cannot be sure whether it is a dream or a visit to Heaven.

THE DREAM

Heaven is a place of great beauty and peace. Everything I see is large and gives the appearance of abundance. The buildings are broad and tall. They are of colors I have never seen before. The fields display beautiful grass and fragrant flowers. The smells and colors are equaled only by the peace that is so prevalent. I feel this peace while here. I also realize I am with someone I know, but his identity remains hidden to me. Arriving is as though we just "popped up" into heaven; entering from a lower level into a setting that is unlike any place I have known in my lifetime. That is how this visitation began. There is no recollection of the trip to get here; we are just suddenly here.

The area we found ourselves in resembles a business park or industrial park. I am very impressed with the size of everything in this industrial area. The buildings are colossal. The atmosphere we find ourselves in is like a fog, though it is not wet or cold. I look off to the right and can see, through the mist, a portion of a large building. The bottom is cement colored and in the shape of an arch. The arch is broad enough to walk or drive through. The arch stands about five stories tall with the rest of the building standing on top of it. The building is so high I cannot see the top of it as it disappears into the clouds. In my spirit, I know that this building stands about 100 floors tall. Observing the size of the building, it is obvious that it was proportionately tall to its length. The width is less than the length and the arch establishes the width size. It is broad enough to have a 10-lane highway pass through the arch. The color of the building is somewhere between orange, red and pink. It is a very impressive building and the color, though dull, is inviting.

I glance to the left and see another tall building. This building is barely visible and looks like a shadow through the fog. It is, however, as large or larger than the building I saw on the right. Glancing straight ahead, I see yet another very tall building, about 80 stories high. This particular building is round and has shield-like metal plates on the side. They have the appearance of the metal nameplates seen on bicycles only these are larger measuring four feet high by six feet wide. These nameplates are attached to, and covering, this entire building along the outside and height of the structure. The shiny metallic plates have some writing on them. I cannot read the words, but I know it is the name of the company. Without a sense of moving, I now find myself on the inside of this round building. Entering one of the rooms, I notice a large quantity of various types of testing equipment. My guides explain to me that the company who owns this building, built it as a launch center for rockets going to other planets and galaxies, yet there are no rockets around. Intuitively, I understand this building to be a training center for individuals as they plan to visit various regions or parts of the universe. Visiting other areas will be possible in Heaven due to our new bodies, and our full understanding of who God is and how He exists. I also understand that the test equipment represents how God measures us as we prepare for eternity.

While still in the dream, I am now out of Heaven and have returned to my test lab on

Earth. As I walk through the laboratory, people are approaching me and asking me many questions about what I learned while visiting this Heavenly laboratory. As I survey my test lab, I recognize some of the same equipment used in the lab in Heaven. In Heaven, I learned how to use the equipment, so now I know how to use this equipment to its fullest potential.

As I wake from this dream or visitation, whatever it is, I am almost disappointed. My heart aches to stay in that place. It was rich with abundance. There were no small buildings, there were no small rooms, everything had the appearance of prosperity, and there was no stress involved in anything. There was no semblance of time as we prepared lessons and test items. Though the buildings were far apart and enormous, walking from one to another was not difficult. I do not remember seeing any doors on the buildings, and yet we entered and left the building easily. It was a gorgeous, relaxing place.

The weather in this place was perfect. It appeared foggy but was very comfortable. The fog reminded me of Genesis and the Garden of Eden. *"But there went up a mist from the earth, and watered the whole face of the ground"* *(Genesis 2:6)*

APPLICATION OR MEANING

Much of this visitation or dream, whichever the case may be, could be highly symbolic. The abundance and size of things I believe are very likely the way things are in Heaven. We serve a God of Abundance. Based on my past experiences, and other people's testimonies, I believe abundance is God's way.

I believe the building with the test equipment represented a teaching center where God uses people to prepare them for Heaven. Yes, I believe we have to prepare for Heaven. The first preparation is to be born-again. Our sinful nature cannot enter Heaven and must be born-again, a transformation of our spirit whereby God performs the miracle of changing us from sinners to saints.

Jesus said that we should go into all the earth and make disciples, leaving us with the work of reaching lost souls. He made it clear that just spreading the Gospel was not enough, but we were also to make disciples. Making disciples takes a team effort with some preaching, some teaching, and some ministering in other ways. No one person is expected, or even encouraged, to try to do it all alone.

The size of the building and the quantity of testing equipment was symbolic of the amount of work, and various gifts humanity needs to get the job done. Coming back to my test lab was symbolic of learning from others and then knowing how to reach out to people on Earth. This process of reaching out to the lost, discipling them, ministering to them, etc. will prepare people for eternity. That is not to say we will not have much to learn when we get to Heaven. I don't know how that process will work. We may automatically know things because we are in Heaven, or we may have all of eternity to learn more and more about Heaven.

There were no rockets to launch because there was no need for them. Once we understand how faith and heavenly living works, we will be able to travel across the universe. I received no further understanding than this. It would be presumptuous to think I have all the answers.

This is what I have learned:

1. When God shows me a house or building it always represents what He is doing in the person. The person is the building or house. The size of the buildings represents the size of the spirit of individuals when getting to Heaven. The amount of test equipment represents the fullness

and understanding of the talents and gifts given by God to individuals when we get to Heaven. I do not think we can even compare who we are now to who we will be in Heaven.

2. There will be meaningful work in Heaven. Just as God told Adam and Eve to tend the Garden, He also has meaningful, or useful, work for us in Heaven.

3. If we believe and accept it, the work we perform here on Earth, can have the same fulfillment as the work we will do in Heaven.

4. Heavenly things can be experienced right here on Earth. When I returned from visiting the Heavenly laboratory, my peers asked me what I had learned. God wants us to ask Him about our work here on Earth so we can learn the Heavenly methods of performing it.

CHAPTER 3

HOUSE DREAMS

"Wherefore, holy brethren, partakers of the heavenly calling, consider the Apostle and High Priest of our profession, Christ Jesus: Who was faithful to him that appointed him, as also Moses was faithful in all his house. For this man was counted worthy of more glory than Moses, inasmuch as he who hath builded the house hath more honour than the house" (Hebrews 3:1-3)

My first house dream was quite remarkable. It took me a while to understand what was happening. I sought The Lord for quite some time to find out what the dream meant. Initially, I thought the dream foretold a house that we were going to purchase. That made me excited since we had two children and were living in a new, yet crowded house of approximately 900 square feet. The search for this house took many months, which eventually turned into years. In the meantime, I was experiencing other dreams and experiences with God. These dreams and experiences made me start to question the actual meaning of the dream. Following are two dreams of the same house. These were my first house dreams.

THE "HUGE HOUSE" DREAM 1

In this dream, I am walking on the roof of an enormous house with multiple rooflines. I am continually moving upward from one roof to another. All these roofs connect to the house and are just additional rooms and sections of the structure. The house seems endless in size, is a beautiful green color, and I feel extremely excited to own this place because of its color and size.

I awoke with a sense of great excitement thinking God is truly going to bless us with a fabulous house, like this one, in which to live. We searched for this house, or one like it, for months without finding a place that seemed to fit the dream. There came over me a great sadness, as I realized that I must have misinterpreted this dream as having come from God.

Then, a new encouragement came to me by way of a second dream of the same house.

THE "HUGE HOUSE" DREAM 2

Setting:

We were planning to drive to Tulsa, Oklahoma from Owatonna, Minnesota to attend a Prophetic Conference. Our only vehicle was an older van we had inherited from Faye's father. It had many miles on it and was not the type of van in which you would want to take your family on a long trip.

Before we left Minnesota, I had another dream:

I am once again walking on the roof of the same multi-level house. On one of the rooftops is an open area where the roof seems to be unfinished and open. The opening goes all the way to the ground. In the center of this opening, and spanning the entire distance, is a linkage joint made up of two pieces of solid, round iron. Each piece has threads on one end that match the threads at the end of the other piece. They are designed and built to assemble just as pipe fittings assemble. When assembled, the length of this linkage is adjustable by turning the threads on one piece into or out of the threads on the other piece. I walk across the linkage noticing the ground is three stories of open space below me. I question myself; why am I walking across the linkage when it is possible just to walk around it? Walking on this narrow linkage terrified me because of its size, and the distance to the floor below. When I was almost finished crossing the linkage, I awoke in a cold sweat. Inside me was a mixture of fear and faith. I knew this time that God was speaking to me, but I still was not sure what He was saying, so I shelved the dream, and we left for Tulsa.

Events after the dream:

The trip was fabulous. We had great ministry time, and the Prophets spoke some very encouraging words over us. This conference provided the beginning of my understanding of dreams and visions. Following this trip, I started remembering many of my dreams from throughout my life. A new person awakened inside of me, and

I could now experience a fuller understanding of who God was and how He worked in our lives.

When we arrived home from this trip, our van suffered a breakdown. The bracket holding the steering linkage to the van's frame broke, and we could not steer the vehicle. That is when I understood the dream and the meaning of the linkage. It was a warning of the dangers facing us as we drove this vehicle. However, God was faithful. He was teaching us how to hear from Him. Like any good teacher, He is patient, allowing us to learn at our pace. He kept us safe as we endeavored to experience more of Him by attending this conference.

APPLICATION OR MEANING

When we arrived home, and the van broke down, He showed me the meaning of the house. The house, He explained, was me. The roof-tops represented seasons, or times, of growth. Therefore, I understood that as I grew in spiritual development, I was moving into a higher and higher understanding of God, and a more personal relationship with Him. He also showed me this was not just for me, but was the experience that every one of His children should be having with Him. Jesus said, *"In my Father's house are many mansions: if it were not so, I would have told you. I go to prepare a place for you" (John 14:2).* He showed me that our mansions are in heaven, but there is also a building process taking place here on earth. There did remain a question in my mind regarding the linkage. Since the house represents me, and the linkage represents the vehicle, what is the connection between the dreams? Again, I asked the Lord, and He showed me that the linkage indeed represented the vehicle, and the house represented me. As the dream showed, there was danger to my family due to the vehicle's condition, but by Gods grace, we remained safe in spite of the danger.

He told me there would be times in my spiritual development where danger existed; sometimes from the enemy trying to destroy the house, and sometimes from gaps or hidden dangers that could cause me to fall. His assurance was that He would be there and guide me safely over those danger spots.

These were only the beginnings of house dreams I experienced. As I grew in understanding, the interpretations came quicker and were more easily understood. However, not all house dreams caused me to awake with a safe and pleasant feeling in my spirit. Some caused me to take a step back and evaluate where I was in my spiritual life. I am also sharing these dreams, for the benefit of those who will listen.

THE ROUND HOUSE

This house was also enormous, round, made of white brick and sat atop a hill. Circling, and built as part of the house, was a six-foot wide corridor. The corridor was enclosed, yet felt open to the outside. As I looked up, it was possible that the roof was pure glass since I could see the sky. As I circled this house, I noticed an abundance of fresh flowers at my side. The aroma, of the flowers, is so soothing; it makes me feel like there is no worry or stress anywhere.

I walked through that corridor, gazing into the house through the many windows on the inside wall. I was totally amazed at how beautiful the inside of the house looked with all its bright and shiny furnishings. I was puzzled as to why I felt I could not get into the house, but could only view it from the corridor through those windows. Looking through the windows, I could see many framed paintings adorning the inside walls. It was truly a peaceful, tranquil, and awe-inspiring place, yet I never entered the house itself. When I awoke, I sensed a feeling of total peace. The smells and colors of the place remained fixed in my mind and my spirit. What a place! I was saddened to wake from this place of tranquility and beauty.

Asking The Lord exactly what this dream meant, I received the following: The house, again, represented me. The corridor represented the path I was currently on in my spiritual development and growth. The corridor seemed not to have a roof and was representative of an open Heaven. What does that mean? It means there is freedom and openness to commune with God as I journey. The pictures and the other elements that comprised the interior of the house, creating its beauty, represent what God is doing in my life. Why couldn't I enter the house? The inside of the house represents my spiritual development, or me. The house represents what God WILL build, or IS building, in me. That is the future. God only reveals as much as we can handle in our time. Daily trusting God will be the building blocks for the future.

APPLICATION OR MEANING

You are also a work in progress. God will guide and direct you every day if you ask Him to be Lord of your life. *"The steps of a good man are ordered by the Lord: and he delighteth in his way" (Psalms 37:23)*

Letting God direct your path and asking Him daily for wisdom and guidance will allow Him to build your spirit and your life until you are complete in Him.

THE MULTI-STORY HOUSE

In this dream, my wife Faye and I entered another huge house. It was made of brick, rect-angular, and stood three floors tall. In the middle of the house was a staircase. Each side of the staircase was open as if the floors and walls didn't exist.

We walked into this house on the first floor. Immediately, I noticed it contained a great number of precious things. Every direction I looked, I saw polished and shiny objects, orna-mental and valuable jewelry, knick-knacks, and many items that I did not recognize, though they were exquisite. Some things sat on the floor, and some sat on shelves. The shelves were glass with bright golden shelf brackets. I walked around the room, gazing upwards and sideways, taking in the beauty and volume of items. There was not one single item out of place. Though the house seemed full of things, it did not have the appearance of clutter or objects infringing upon each other.

There were thousands of things in this house; yet, there was plenty of room for it all. There appeared to be lots of room for more things while leaving very little room for anything more. It was like being famished and having eaten too much at the same time. It was unsettling and relaxing at the same time. As I walked around, I somehow knew that all these items, and the house, belonged to us. It was as if we lived there but had never been there before. Only God could help us make sense of this. We walked the stairway to the second floor, and I saw more of the same. There were shelves with golden brackets. The shelves were full of beautiful and precious items. There were also pieces on the floor. Thousands of pieces: none of them was infringing on another's space. The room appeared to be full, with little or no space available to hold more items, while still leaving the appearance of space available for more. The feeling of awe was so overwhelming that I was not sure I could remain standing.

Then we walked to the third floor. It was like the first and second floors, filled with many shiny and beautiful objects. I remember feeling great prosperity from owning this place with all these bright and fancy things. Since the center of the house contained all these things, I thought the bedrooms would also contain an abundance of bright and valuable objects. I wondered if there would be so much stuff that there would not be room to sleep. We never found out, since we didn't see the area outside of the spacious rooms around the staircase. It was as if there was no need for a bedroom, kitchen, or living room. We also noticed that there was no furniture visible. All we could see were things all around us.

Suddenly, I found myself standing outside, in front of an open garage door, looking into an extremely dark space. It was a standard two car attached garage. As I looked toward the front of the garage, I noticed the floor sloped downward, eventually disappearing into total darkness. It was scary to say the least. The entire inside of the garage disappeared into total blackness within a few feet of the doorway. My imagination was running wild as I pictured what might be in there. Was it full of bats? Were mice and rates abundant in there? If I went in there, would wild animals like skunks or raccoons attack me? What if I stumbled and fell. Would anyone know? Perhaps I would get seriously hurt or even die. My mind was running wild with misadventures from going into this dark and spooky place. Then I awoke.

APPLICATION OR MEANING

The message was immediate. Even before I awoke, I realized the meaning of this dream. God was building a beautiful structure. All of God's buildings are beautiful. The structure, or house, again represented my spiritual life. I cannot say that the house was complete to that stage; however, it was a symbol of what God was doing and what the outcome would be.

The shiny items in the house represented two things. They were things we accumulate and seek after more than we seek after God. These things can, and often do, rob our attention of God. They also represent the blessings of God. They may be gifts and talents given to individuals or may be God's blessings for us to enjoy. The difference in these symbols all has to do with the heart. Is your heart seeking and accumulating worldly goods; or is your heart seeking and accumulating God's best for you?

The stairway seemed significant. It represents our upward walk as we grow in knowledge and understanding of God. As we grow and progress, we achieve gifts, represented by the many things in the rooms. When the house is complete, we go to Heaven. There is no need for furniture, beds, bedrooms, kitchens, etc. in Heaven. God is our source. These rooms and furnishings are only valid while journeying on Earth.

The garage represents an area, or areas, of my life that are still under construction. Some of these areas are so dark that there is little or no light shining on them. These things still need work. It is not that I am not saved and going to Heaven, but they are areas that still need improvement. I compare it to when the children of Israel entered the Promised Land. God, through Moses, spoke to them telling them that they would not occupy the whole land immediately. Rather, they would fight for the land and take as much (be given as much, by God) as they could inhabit and tend to. There is a reason for not receiving all the land at once. God said if He drove out the inhabitants too quickly, the wild animals would become too great for the people. *"And the Lord thy God will put out those nations before thee by little and little: thou mayest not consume them at once, lest the beasts of the field increase upon thee" (Deuteronomy 7:22)*

We all have areas (habits, weaknesses, etc.) that need improvement. Though we think our house is gorgeous, well kept, and clean, there are still areas where we all struggle. Seeking God daily and allowing Him to clean and decorate the house and garage, will make us into an image of Him. When our time comes to meet Him, then we can hear Him say, "Well done thou good and faithful servant."

WOODEN FRAMEWORK HOUSE

This house was brand new construction. The entire framework was set up, but there was no sheetrock, no ceilings and not even a roof on the structure. Even without ceilings, there were floors that we could walk on. We were walking around in the house as if we lived there. On the second level, there was a small open space much like a large closet. It had a floor but no walls, and yet it seemed very tiny. It had the appearance of a landing just off the stairway. On this landing was a copy machine. I remember approaching the copy machine as if to make copies, but something felt odd, even spooky, about this machine. It was not fear I felt but rather an apprehension. As I stood next to the machine to make copies, suddenly a great rainstorm began. Since there was no roof on the house, the rain was free to pour in on us. I felt sick over how the rain would ruin the structure of the house and would ruin the copy machine. The dream ended here.

APPLICATION OR MEANING

Every believer starts with a framework structure. God "builds" us spiritually as we walk with Him and study His Word. This frame house represents the solidness of our relationship with Jesus when we are born-again. Again, I believe this dream was a word to me regarding my spiritual life. It could also apply to many of you. I had already seen in my dreams, many times, the huge nearly completed houses. So why all of a sudden did I have this dream about the frame only and what was the copy machine about?

The Lord showed me that we will not be complete in Him nor will our mansion (house) will be complete until we get to heaven. In the meantime, there will be seasons in our life where we may not be walking in the perfect will of God as we should be. These seasons come about as we work through the trials of life. Jesus said that we would have trials here on earth, but He also said that we should not worry because

He has overcome the world. *"These things I have spoken unto you, that in me ye might have peace. In the world ye shall have tribulation: but be of good cheer; I have overcome the world"* (John 16:33)

In the midst of these trials, the message is this: The framework, or the house structure, is intact. I have counseled many people who have been afraid that they have lost their salvation because they had a setback. This setback may have been returning to an addiction they were so confident they had broken. It could also be a secret sin, one they had struggled with for years. It may even be a temptation that just pops up, is given into, and the result is sin.

The message is this: we live in a fallen world. We all struggle with temptation. We're all pressured by the enemy, the world, and our flesh to gratify the desires of the flesh. When we, in our weakness, succumb to temptation, it does not mean that we have lost our salvation. Our framework is stable but weakened by sin. The framework, our soul, and spirit, is built on a rock. That rock is Jesus Christ. Your occasional yield to temptation does not destroy the structure of what God is doing in you. There certainly is a need to repent when we backslide or fall into sin, but God will take that failure and continue to build the house. He may even use that experience as a part of the house. Just repent and believe God for forgiveness and go on allowing God to build more.

Regarding the copy machine, God showed me that too many of His children are either preaching or teaching that there is only one way to serve God. This preaching results from a spirit of pride. God gives every person a gift or gifts. Only God can direct and tell that person how to use their gift(s). I urge you to find out what your gift is and use it as God leads. He also showed me that people are prophesying other people's prophecies and calling themselves prophets. This practice has to stop. When we say, "Thus says The Lord," God takes that seriously. He does not want to be misquoted, and He does not want people stealing His words from other children. We are not copies of anyone. We are each made unique and have unique gifts for the body. If you have a word of Prophecy, then share it. If it is a word you have heard, or received, then give credit to the person who received it from God. Remember: Use your gift in the way God directs you.

I have experienced this. I nearly failed Bible School Homiletics because I had trouble structuring the sermons in the way outlined by the instructor. I had been a student of Billy Graham most of my life. I watched and studied him. At the age of nine, I started preaching to the trees and the cows on our dairy farm in Wisconsin. I became fully convinced that I could "hold a crowd in the palms of my hands". What I mean by that is this; I could keep their attention, build a case for salvation and lead them to a relationship with Jesus.

By the time I started Bible School, I had preached dozens of sermons, in numerous churches and other settings. When I got into the homiletics course and tried to write a sermon the way the instructor taught us, I stumbled and grasped for words as I attempted to follow the outline as presented. Following a prescribed method is good, but it is better to follow God's way as He directs you by His Holy Spirit.

I have worked in the field of Quality Control in engineering companies inspecting the work produced from Engineer's drawings or blueprints. I know, for a part to work to its optimum benefit, the part has to be made per the engineer's specification as drawn on the blueprint. God's blueprint for your life works in much the same way. That blueprint includes gifts and callings. Do it God's way and you will not be disappointed.

When God gives you a gift, only HE can direct its use. HE developed it. HE designed it.

HE gave it. Seek God's direction for its use. Do not try to copy someone else's design. We were in a Prophetic Conference in Fort Mills, SC. One of the speakers conveyed a story about an individual who was trying to imitate the speaker's prophetic gift. This speaker was teaching us that God has a special gift and talent for each of us. His words were, "stay out of my mantra". In other words, use your God-given gift in the way God directs.

That does not mean that there is not a time for study and learning. There certainly is a time for study and learning. There is also a time for practicing and receiving Godly wisdom. Nevertheless, none of us can afford to have this training or mentoring cause us to lose sight of the gifting God has placed in us. It is the same Holy Spirit, but different administrations of the gifts, which complete the body of Christ. *"And there are differences of administrations, but the same Lord" (1 Corinthians 12:5)*

If God has given you the ability to preach, then preach according to the Faith given you. *"So we, being many, are one body in Christ, and every one members one of another. Having then gifts differing according to the grace that is given to us, whether prophecy, let us prophesy according to the proportion of faith; Or ministry, let us wait on our ministering: or he that teacheth, on teaching"* (Romans 12:5-7)

If your gift is to paint, then paint according to the gift inside of you. If your gift is to make money and distribute it then do it as God has shown you to do it. You are not a copy of someone else. No one else has the exact, same gifting and calling that you have. Do not pick out a person and say they are the one I am going to be like. I thought for years; I will be like Billy Graham, traveling around the world preaching crusades. Then God showed me a new way. My gifting is different than Billy Graham has and yet is very similar.

To illustrate this point, I will give an example from my experiences. I was preaching an evangelistic message in a small church in southern Minnesota. I gave an altar call and this young man, about 14-15 years old, came to the altar. This young man lived in a God-fearing household, attending church regularly. He said he was having issues with demons. He also said that he enjoyed playing the game Dungeons and Dragons. He had tried many times to stop playing but said it was as if a hand reached out and dragged him to the game. He just was not capable of stopping. His prayer was for deliverance from the game.

I turned my back on him to seek God's direction for prayer. When I turned around, he was right in front me with his fists raised to my face. The look in his eyes told me that if I backed down he would hurt me badly. I laid my hands on his stomach (representative of his spirit) and commanded the demons to let him lose "in Jesus Name"! He buckled over at his waist and moaned a horrible sound that nearly made the hair stand up on my neck. Then he stood upright, growled at me with bare teeth and shoved his fists up to my face again. This scenario repeated itself many times, as other people in the congregation came forward with words of knowledge regarding this young man. They would come forward and tell me of different spirits in operation in this young man. Each time we declared the spirits name, the young man would bend over and moan hideously. We cast thirteen spirits out of him that night. After expelling the final named spirit, he came charging at me. I thought, Oh no! He is going to attack me. He did attack me, but not in the way I supposed it would be. He grabbed my neck and hugged me so tightly I was barely able to breath. I understand that this boy, now a grown man, is preaching the Gospel and delivering people from Satan's grasp. God can use different people with the same gifts uniquely. Billy Graham and I both preach evangelistically, but God uses our gifts in a different way and different administrations.

Whatever your gift is, do it according to God's direction. The Word of God says that your gift will make room for itself. *"A man's gift maketh room for him, and bringeth him before great men" (Proverbs 18:16)*

My advice for each person reading or hearing this message is just to keep following God and believing that He will open the doors. As you use your gift, do not try to imitate someone else. You may glean or learn from them, but your gift may work differently in a different setting or for a different purpose.

HOUSE WITH LEAKING ROOF

This house was not new. We were living in the house, but we were not happy living there. We wanted something nicer and newer. We were in total discontent with our living situation. The house seemed to provide no rest while we were there and was a horrible place to return to when we came home.

Every time it rained, the roof would leak, and the ceilings would be wet from one end to the other. The ceiling had large holes where the plaster had fallen. The rafters and roof were visible through these openings. When it rained, water ran down the walls loosening the wallpaper. The entire structure appeared as if it might fall. We did not have the money or means to fix the roof and correct the problem. It was a terrible feeling to be in the house. We felt like we were in a situation where we had no control over the weather or the leakage. It just seemed like we were in prison.

APPLICATION OR MEANING

Rain can be a symbol of good or bad in our lives. Without the rain, no crop would grow. Too much rain and it causes flooding. Rain into a house is dangerous since it can destroy the structure. Our houses need to be weather proofed.

God was showing me a time in my life where I was struggling with my spiritual walk. The roof, or covering, was in a state of disrepair. What does that mean? I was walking outside of God's plan and purpose in my life. I became back-slidden and not seeking God through prayer and study. I was walking out of the covering of God's protection. Probably most of us have those seasons in life, seasons when we get overwhelmed with the cares of the world and end up neglecting God. The Bible warns that the cares of this world can choke out the Word of God. *"And the cares of this world, and the deceitfulness of riches, and the lusts of other things entering in, choke the word, and it becometh unfruitful"* (Mark 4:19)

God does not forget nor neglect us. He promises in His Word that He will never leave us nor forsake us. *"Let your conversation be without covetousness; and be content with such things as ye have: for he hath said, I will never leave thee, nor forsake thee"* (Hebrews 13:5)

Thankfully, God has a way of getting our attention. For me, it is through house dreams. If you find yourself in the situation where life seems to be leaking rain into your house, do these things:

1. Seek God
2. Ask Forgiveness
3. Take time daily to pray and read His Word, asking Him to open its contents and meanings to reveal to you how it fits your life and your situation.

God still gives me dreams now and then about a leaking roof. I hate those dreams. They are a stark reminder that I am not following Him and spending time with Him. In God's Word we read, the ones He loves He disciplines. *"Now no chastening for the present seemeth to be joyous, but grievous: nevertheless afterward it yieldeth the peaceable fruit of righteousness unto them which are exercised thereby"* (Hebrews 12:11). No discipline is comfortable for the moment, but it will lead us into a better path and a better life. Many of us grew up knowing what a switch or belt was. It was often used for discipline. I understand that, far too often, the punishment turns to abuse, and I do not condone that. The Bible says, *"In the lips of him that hath understanding wisdom is found: but a rod is for the back of him that is void of understanding"* (Proverbs 10:13)

Most of the younger parents I know use time-outs or some less extreme measure of discipline. It is not my intent to teach on proper discipline here, but it is my intent to make you aware that

God disciplines those He loves. Every person needs teaching on right from wrong. We call it boundaries. God gave the Ten Commandments, so we would understand what the boundaries are, and so we would understand that we are not holy enough to enter His kingdom. God's discipline will always lead a person to the proper path, and to God Himself. God always has our best interest at heart when He disciplines us, no matter how hard or harsh that discipline seems.

When it seems that the cares (rains) of life are damaging our life, that is the time to seek God in prayer regarding what is happening. These times of rain are not necessarily times of discipline or failure. God will show us the meaning of the rain, whether it is damaging our house or watering the fields if we ask Him for the purpose. If we are outside His will, He will work whatever is necessary to get us back into His will.

MULTI-LEVEL HOUSE WITH
UNFINISHED ROOMS

This dream was of a house in a neighborhood where the structures stand very close together. Although the development was still under construction, and far from finished, we had moved into our house. This house was four stories, but quite small. The structure was sitting on wooden pilings, had a wooden framework, no basement, with the floor one foot off the ground. You could look right underneath the house and see to the other side, except in the places where the view was obstructed by piles of dirt left under the house. It was obvious that this wood structure was not pressure treated in any way and would quickly rot over time. There was no preparation to the land or the pilings before placing the house on these pilings.

Inside the house, very few walls were completed. To enter the bedrooms, we had to jump onto a plywood floor and pull ourselves up. From there we had to crawl on our hands and knees to get from one room to an-other. The floors were all plywood with most floors sagging and unsteady. As we crawled from room to room, the floors would bounce and nearly cave-in under our weight. Approaching the back of the house, where most of the bedrooms were, the floors became increasingly uneven and sagged. Each room held multiple piles of dirt, and the rooms became darker and darker as we went further into the house and entered several bedrooms.

As often happens in these dreams, I suddenly found myself outside. Neighbors were walking by using shovels to poke at the structure and digging in the dirt under the house. On the street close by, many cars were parked along the curb. People were coming from the street carrying shovels. They stopped at our place and shoveled dirt from under the house into buckets. In my spirit, I was experiencing strong feelings of being violated, and embarrassment, because of how bad the house looked. I was amazed that people were so interested in our house and angered that they would steal from us right before our eyes. I was also concerned about any damage they may be causing the structure of the house as they removed dirt from underneath it.

APPLICATION OR MEANING

Sometimes we get ahead of God. While He is building us into a structure, or person, that will be strong and usable to Him, we get a glimpse of the vision being prepared for us and just take over the building process. Moving into the wooden structure that has a poor foundation represents this. We have the basic design, represented by the various rooms, but no room is complete because we only have a glimpse of what we are to become. We move from place to place, represented by the rooms, and we do not allow the Lord to complete the process in each area. By spending time with God each day, and learning to hear His voice, we can confidently make the necessary moves or adjustments required for the finishing of the house and its rooms.

The neighbors represent Christians around us who do not understand what God is doing in our lives. They criticize and mock the structure; not being aware that in so doing they are mocking what God is doing in their lives and ours. Taking the dirt is symbolic of the damage this causes. Parts of our growth become lost when people steal what God is building. Those items taken may be the special gift or portion of a gift God is developing in us. Stealing these gifts happens when someone thinks they know what is best for you. They interfere with the process by advising or teaching how they think you should do something or how they think you should use your gift. Once again, if God has given you a gift or talent, seek Him, and He will direct you in its use. Stay in communion with God for His direction. *"Trust in the Lord with all thine heart; and lean not unto thine own understanding. In all thy ways acknowledge him, and he shall direct thy paths" (Proverbs 3:5-6)*

The passersby represent the world's population trying to get what we have to offer as Christians. They have not come to a place where they are repenting and asking God for salvation, but they recognize something that we have and want a portion of it. An improperly laid foundation on God's Word (The Bible) can cause suffering from what these people take out of our lives. We can also suffer from the negative words and thoughts they leave behind.

So our main application here is this: do not get ahead of God. Allow Him to complete the building process one room at a time. When the Children of Israel entered the Promised Land, God did not give them the entire land all at once. He said that, if He gave it all to them at once, the land would become overgrown and full of wild animals. *"And the Lord thy God will put out those nations before thee by little and little: thou mayest not consume them at once, lest the beasts of the field increase upon thee" (Deuteronomy 7:22)*

Learn from this. God will allow the world to cultivate and prosper while you are growing. At the fullness of time, He will give you a harvest where you have not planted. God will allow someone to cultivate and till the ground that He will someday give to you. That way you do not have to start the planting process over and over by trying to till ground that is hard and barren. Some of this cultivating, planting and harvest is spiritual, and some may be physical. You may lead individuals, ministered to by many others, to Christ because you happen to be there at the right time. You may also receive wealth or goods from people who have worked hard to gain it, and God instructs them to give it to you. It may come as an inheritance or as a total surprise gift. It may be an opportunity for a good job or a good education. Protect what the Lord has given you. Do not let others steal what God intends for you.

WOODEN STRUCTURE HOUSE WITH HORRIBLE BASEMENT

This house dream was much like the last dream. The house was in the process of construction and had a very strong foundation. The inside of the house had sheetrock walls in place, but the walls remained unpainted. The house was not very big, maybe 1000 square feet, and yet the rooms seemed very large. It was quite comfortable. In the center of the living room floor was a large hole with a plywood cover over it. Removing the plywood and looking into the hole, we could see that it was a large area under the house. It could qualify as a basement, but seemed more like a dungeon. It was very deep and very dark. In spite of the darkness, I was able to see many things lying all over the floor.

There were three of us looking into this dungeon. One of the other people was my brother, but I did not see the third person's face. We placed a tall ladder into the hole, and two of us climbed down the ladder while my brother stayed in the living room watching us. We were in an unusual and different area. It was dark, yet light enough to see our way around and identify objects within the space. It was an eerie feeling being in this area. It felt like there was a presence of something in the space-something we could not immediately identify. The further we walked away from the ladder the darker the room became. Many objects were lying on the floor, but we could not identify any of them. There seemed to be pieces of junk or shrapnel everywhere. This room was definitely not a room in which we wanted to stay. I thought, "This is a beautiful house, but we will not be coming back into the basement." Then the dream ended.

APPLICATION OR MEANING

Once again, we find a house that is under construction. As God builds us into a strong dwelling place for His Spirit to inhabit, only portions of the house get finished at a time.

In this case, the hurts and bad experiences from the past, represented by the shrapnel in the basement, are pushed down, (into our spirits) and instead of being dealt with are ignored. The house continues being constructed, and it is glorious. But the junk, (bad experiences, bad habits, mistakes, false accusations, etc.), often end up in the basement (our souls and spirits), where we hide it. Nevertheless, inside we always know it is there.

I sense God telling us to deal appropriately with issues as they develop or resolve them as quickly as we can. If we do not deal with these issues, we continue building our houses over a pile of accumulating junk. The large space indicated that the bad experiences, the mistakes, the false accusations, etc. would always be happening to us or around us. By continually ignoring these issues and tossing them into the large cavity, we eventually have more to deal with than we can handle.

Throwing the junk into the cavity is our equivalent of "stuffing" issues into our spirits and not properly dealing with them. Dealing with them may involve giving forgiveness, seeking forgiveness, discussing hurts or working through hurtful events. These are only a few suggestions. There are many opportunities for hurt and stuffing. We need to identify these areas and deal with them immediately. Unfortunately, if not properly dealt with, all this stuffing of issues may manifest itself as sickness, anger, depression, acts of rage or even murder. The cavity is large because it represents our life and our lifetime. Be careful what you allow to fill this cavity over your lifetime. Things you think do not matter, or that you think are gone, may someday come out and manifest themselves in hideous or horrible ways. Too much junk can ruin a life. Be quick to forgive for your sake as well as for those who harm you. *"For if ye forgive men their trespasses, your heavenly Father will also forgive you" (Matthew 6:14)*

LIVING WITH MOM IN OLD HOUSE

In my dreams, it is usually Dad representing our Heavenly Father. I will illustrate more in later dreams. Since God is All in All, it should not be strange that He would reveal himself as a mother as well as a father. This concept seemed strange to me until one night I dreamt about my Mom instead of my Dad. The house we lived in was quite old and furnished with old appliances and old furniture. It was a short dream, but the message was plain.

From my upstairs bedroom, I came down the stairway and into the kitchen. The stove sat against a wall on the far end of the kitchen. The staircase was behind this wall and only visible from one corner of the kitchen, and not visible from any other room downstairs. The location and visibility of the staircase seemed quite important in the dream. I walked to the front of the house and turned around to look towards the stairway. The structure of the house resembled an old one-room schoolhouse, being open from front to back with only one room visible, which included the living room and kitchen. Covering the walls was mass quantities of old wallpaper that had been outdated decades ago. The wallpaper was peeling and yellowed from years of exposure to cooking and sunlight. Everything in this house, including the furniture and the appliances, was old and rundown.

Standing just inside the front door, looking toward the kitchen, I could see the entire first floor of the house. The ceiling was high with exposed beams leading to the peaks. The kitchen was at the far end of the house. There was a large clock mounted on the kitchen wall facing the front door. The clock also seemed to be important in the dream. Directly behind the kitchen wall was the stairway leading upstairs. The stairway was not visible from where I was standing. However, I had just come down those stairs, so I was aware of their existence. The visibility of the stairs seems quite important in

the dream, but I have not received any interpretation regarding the stairway location. As I
stood looking toward the back of the house, my
attention focused on the clock. I could not make
out what time it read, but something about the
clock made me uncomfortable. It was a huge
clock with a face about thirty-six inches in diam-
eter with very large hands. As I was studying
the clock, a bat flew out of the stairway and
came toward me. With the bat flying toward her,
but behind her, Mom came running toward me
and said, "I hate this house. It is so old and
uncomfortable I just want something better."
The expression on her face was not a look of
anger but rather a look of disappointment and
frustration.

When I woke from this dream, the emotions
I felt were nearly overwhelming. I was so sad
for my mom that she felt that way. I was somewhat upset at my dad for not providing a better
house for Mom. I fought back the feelings of
anger and disappointment towards my Dad and

fought back the tears of sadness I felt for my Mom. It took me a few moments to realize this was just a dream.

As I was meditating and working through my emotions regarding the dream, I realized that I needed to ask God if there was a spiritual significance to the dream and if so, what was it. Then The Holy Spirit revealed to me that Mom was also representing God in my dream.

The interpretation given to me was this:

Once again, the house represents me. My house had begun to deteriorate due to lack of maintenance. To keep our spiritual house maintained and in proper order, we must daily spend time reading God's Word and spend time communicating with God, praying and listening. The old house represented my attitude towards this maintenance. I had become comfortable in the things that I had learned and studied from the past. Without the regular maintenance of God's Word, the house had become old and infested with bats. The bats represented the destructive habits and attitudes of this world that come to steal the Word from us. Left alone these bats (habits) will destroy and occupy the house. God (Mom) was not happy with how my house had become. It had nothing to do with my earthly mom being hurt and unhappy. Instead, it had everything to do with my Heavenly Mom (God). I believe God used my mom in this dream to show the soft side of God's love to me in spite of my neglect of the house. In our western civilization, the woman is the heart of the home. God showed me His heart toward my house (my being) by using my mom to speak to me in this dream.

The clock represents time. The size and large hands represent how quickly time passes. The large face is a calling to spend time with Him. Due to the lateness of time in history, the size of the clock represents the largeness of urgency for spending quality time with Him.

APPLICATION OR MEANING

Neglecting God in prayer or in reading The Word can cause our lives to become infested with unwanted things. Things like sickness, poverty, loneliness, etc. God has a better plan for our lives than these listed items. It is the enemy, the devil, who causes hurts and destructive things to enter our lives. God only has good things for us. *"The thief cometh not, but for to steal, and to kill, and to destroy: I am come that they might have life, and that they might have it more abundantly" (John 10:10)*

The thief enters our house when we open the door to him. The door opens when we neglect God's word and when we neglect prayer. Watching evil programs or movies; listening to ungodly music, hanging out in places that are influenced by the devil, spending too much time with and allowing people of the world to influence our words and decisions. All these things and more will allow the enemy to enter our houses and destroy the structure. It may not seem like a once in awhile sin (like viewing a porn site or watching a suggestive TV program) is causing any damage, but the truth is, behavior like that will give the devil a foothold in your life. The sin is like an addiction. It grows bigger and bigger until what we thought were "little sins" are now gross habits and attitudes. If a person continues in this pattern of sin, slowly and surely the enemy will cause your house structure to become unstable and destroyed. That is not to say a person will lose their salvation, but destroying the temple of The Holy Spirit (our body) could result in the death of the body through sickness, accident or even murder. *"What? know ye not that your body is the temple of the Holy Ghost which is in you, which ye have of God, and ye are not your own? For ye are bought with a price: therefore glorify God in your body, and in your spirit, which are God's"* *(1 Corinthians 6:19-20)*

Our emphasis here has to be on spending time with God. Spending time with God will result in proper talking, proper behavior, proper worship, and proper praise of our Savior. If you feel your house is suffering from lack of Holy Spirit, and you notice the world having more influence over you than it should, then it is time to repent and get closer to God. Praying and reading the Bible are the keys to a fulfilled and happy life.

TEN STORY BUILDING IN HEAVEN

"It is not expedient for me doubtless to glory. I will come to visions and revelations of the Lord. I knew a man in Christ above fourteen years ago, (whether in the body, I cannot tell; or whether out of the body, I cannot tell: God knoweth;) such an one caught up to the third heaven. And I knew such a man, (whether in the body, or out of the body, I cannot tell: God knoweth;) 2 Corinthians 12:1-3

Like Paul, I do not know if this was a dream or if I, in the spirit, visited heaven. One thing I know about seeing heaven is that I always seem to pop up when I get there. It is as if I travel upward and suddenly appear in a completely different environment.

In this case, my escort is a heavenly being who was totally dressed in white. This being, which I believe to be an angel, took me to a city and showed me a special building. We seemed to just pop-up above clouds and enter the city. In the city were many people I recognized. My mom and dad were there, my grandparents and numerous friends that I had known since childhood. When I visited this city, my parents were still alive on earth, which makes me think this may have been a dream, not a visitation. Only God knows for sure.

As I popped up into this city, my attention immediately went to a ten-story building. The building appeared to be a glass office building, the style as we have in cities here on earth. The blue colored glass reflected the light from the outside, but at night, it was possible to see the lights coming from inside the building. As I entered the building, I recognized many of the people already inside. They gathered around and welcomed me, telling me how great a house God is building in which I would live. The entire center of the building from the third floor up was like a hollow tube. Each floor had an already prepared walkway along the outside edge of the tube and circling around the center of the floor. My escort took me to the fifth floor of the building.

From the fifth floor, we could look down on the work that was taking place in the house. Working below us, on the third floor, was huge earth moving equipment: bulldozers and Caterpillar trucks carrying tons of earth. It resembles a scene of a massive road construction project or what you might see at a mining operation; only it was taking place in this beautiful ten-story building that will be my house.

I immediately received in my spirit the interpretation of this event. God was working a grand plan in my life. To give you the best understanding of what this meant, I am going to give you a personal testimony of our life since answering the call to ministry.

THE CALL

I was thirty years old when I answered the call to ministry. Faye and I had just recently repented of our sin and had given our hearts and our life to Jesus. Nine months later, after receiving The Holy Spirit into our lives and dedicating our lives to God and His service, I lost my job due to downsizing. I was out of work for thirteen months. Faye was a stay at home mom at the time. She holds a degree in Social Work, but we had made the decision that she would be at home for the children. We wanted our children to come home from school to a home where mom was there to listen to them and give them the nurture they required.

During the thirteen months, I was off work, Faye, and I did whatever we could to make a few dollars. Faye took a part-time job while I worked at odd jobs to make ends meet. We never quit tithing during this season of our life. God was faithful. We did not get sick. We never went without food, shelter, or clothing, while always managing to keep up with our payments. Another benefit of this period was the amount of time I spent with our pastor. I shadowed him everywhere his ministry duties took him: to nursing homes, hospitals, Bible studies, church plantings, etc. Wherever he ministered, I was there to learn from him. During this time, the congregation voted to install me as the head elder of the congregation. When this pastor and his family accepted a call to another city, the elders' board blessed me by allowing me to fill in as interim pastor at our church. I was even asked to remain as the full-time pastor, but I declined, saying I was not ready and needed to attend Bible school.

That one event set in motion another fifteen year period of seeking God and stepping out in faith multiple times to attend Bible school. During this fifteen-year journey, we experienced many job losses and setbacks. Numerous times, we gave up jobs, houses, family, and friends to follow the path on which God was directing us. We did eventually complete Bible school. It was not the school I anticipated attending, but it was Bible teaching and was definitely of God. A later section of this book, titled The Keys, will discuss the dream I had regarding this school and church.

Back to the dream:

When I saw the ten-story building and all the construction that was taking place, I knew God was doing a special work in my life. Since He was only on the third floor, I knew there was much to come to build ten floors. The path we have been on to get to the third floor involved many hardships and tears, and I wondered how we would make it to the tenth floor. However, God has always been faithful to His Word. We look forward to the building of the remaining floors. If God ordains it, we will pay any price to complete it.

A final thought on the dirt. Building a building involves moving a lot of land and earth. Many of us have habits, failures, or sins from the past as represented by the dirt. Our sins, though forgiven, may leave behind dirt or leftovers needing removal. Only God can do that. The heavy equipment represents the amount of effort required to remove the past dirt. This dirt was inside the building. That means there may still be sins and attitudes in our hearts that need cleaning or removal. I leave that to God. Only Jesus' blood can cleanse us and purify us.

APPLICATION OR MEANING

God is doing a work in each of us. Only He knows how the finished product will look. I suffered from low self-esteem all my life. Low self-esteem is some of the dirt God is removing. Some of the setbacks we face are definitely from the enemy while others are a result of decisions or choices we have made. Many of those decisions are the result of the low self-esteem.

God can remove all the old dirt from our lives. Just give it to Him and He will remove it all. Having suffered low self-esteem almost my whole life, by showing me this building, God raised my self-esteem, so I can go forth and serve Him better.

God will and may already be building you into a bigger building. Pride should not be the result. A bigger building just means that you are called to do something more for God. If He has to remove dirt from your house as He builds it, then let Him do it. You will benefit greatly, in this life and in the life to come, if you just allow God to build you into what He wants you to be.

CHAPTER 4

MY DAD IN DREAMS REPRESENTS GOD THE FATHER

In chapter one, we discussed how God uses other people that we know to represent particular groups or individuals as He communicates with us in dreams. In my dreams, God uses my earthly dad to represent my Heavenly Father. He also uses my siblings to represent brothers and sisters in Christ.

Following are dreams where God has used my earthly dad to represent my Heavenly Father.

Some of these dreams are a combination of houses and dad.

THE TRIP

"And as he journeyed, he came near Damascus: and suddenly there shined round about him a light from heaven: And he fell to the earth, and heard a voice saying unto him, Saul, Saul, why persecutest thou me? And he said, Who art thou, Lord? And the Lord said, I am Jesus whom thou persecutest: it is hard for thee to kick against the pricks. And he trembling and astonished said, Lord, what wilt thou have me to do? And the Lord said unto him, Arise, and go into the city, and it shall be told thee what thou must do" (Acts 9:3-6)

The background setting:

This dream will make more sense with some understanding of what was happening in our life at this time. Faye and I had a Damascus Road type of experience with Jesus. We did not audibly hear the voice of Jesus or have our eyes blinded as Saul did on the road to Damascus. However, we did have a supernatural experience where the Holy Spirit came upon us revealing to us a need for a Savior and we were Born-Again. We then recognized that we were sinners on our way to hell. Repenting of our sin, we asked Jesus to be the Lord of our lives. I will be referring to this experience with God as our conversion or as "being saved" in later paragraphs.

This life-changing experience prompted us to find a Bible teaching, Jesus preaching church. We visited a church one Sunday night only to find that the congregation had canceled the Sunday night services. Next to the church was a house. We went to the door of the house, rang the doorbell, and a tall, mustached cowboy answered the door. His name was Dave. I asked him if he knew anything about the church next door. He said he sure did and that he was the pastor of the church. He invited us in and introduced us to his wife and two children. They had a daughter who was the same age as our daughter and a son who was the same age as our son. This Sunday night meeting turned into a great friendship between our families, which turned out to be invaluable to our family. Nine months following our conversion, the company I worked for downsized, and I was laid off from my job. I was out of work for thirteen months. I spent as much of this time as I could with Pastor Dave being mentored and trained for ministry work while attending off-campus studies through The Berea School of the Bible.

When I went back to work after thirteen months, I continued working with Pastor Dave as much as I could. I was jubilant when the congregation installed me as the head elder of the church. I enjoyed the work of elder and had earned the respect of men twice my age. Then the unexpected happened. Pastor Dave accepted a call to another church, leaving me with what I can only de-scribe as, a feeling of confusion and despair in my soul. I had such mixed emotions about him leaving. I wanted what was best for him and his family, of course, yet I felt like my training was not complete, and I wondered how I was to finish it.

After Pastor Dave and his family had moved, I asked permission of the elders to preach the next Sunday, to which they readily agreed. By this time, preaching came easily for me. Pastor Dave had me visiting and preaching in other churches as well as nursing homes, campgrounds, and private homes. I prepared and presented this sermon with the greatest vigor I had ever put into a sermon. I was, after all, preaching to my friends and peers in my home church.

I must have done quite well because I continued to preach at our church for another six months. I was also performing the tasks of the Pastor, except for weddings and funerals, since I was not licensed to carry out these sacraments. I also continued the tasks of the head elder. We had a call in for a new pastor, and many Pastors came to visit and minister to our congregation.

I even received a call from some of the members of the congregation asking me to be the pastor. At this point in my training, I did not feel ready and turned them down. I did continue to perform the work of pastor and elder until we hired a new pastor.

Part of the work I performed included assisting the local Assembly of God Church with baptism. They held this service on Sunday night at our church. They met in a storefront church and, therefore, had no baptismal. Our baptismal was a water tank under the altar in the front of the church. We filled the water tank from the water heater located in the back of the church. Filling the tank was no easy task. To prepare the baptismal tank with temperate water, we had to run water through a hose from the water heater in the back of the church to the tank in the front of the church. The water heater would run out of hot water and require about one to two hours to heat more water. Since we lived about twelve miles from the church, I remained at the church following the Sunday morning service. I filled the baptismal tank by draining the water heater of hot water, then allowing it to heat more water. I repeated this process repeatedly throughout the day. This process allowed the visiting church to hold their baptism service in our church on Sunday evening in a warm baptismal tank.

The first baptism I prepared for the visiting church was quite an event for me. I stayed for the baptismal service and witnessed a move of God that I never experienced, and yet had felt was real since I was a child. They were speaking in tongues, giving prophecy, words of knowledge along with praise and worship. I felt alive in this service. I knew that I was exactly where I was supposed to be, and this made me feel very comfortable. I am now part of a move of God, that God had shown me in my spirit as a youth, but that I had never witnessed first-hand.

My curiosity overflowed and as soon as it was possible, I sat down for a meeting with the pastor from that church. He explained, using Scripture, what they were doing and why. That service and meeting moved me deeply and awakened my spirit to what God was telling me. I thought of the disciples on their way to Emmaus following the crucifixion of Jesus. In Luke 24:32, it is said, their hearts burned within them at the sound of His voice. That is how I felt at this baptismal service. I knew then that I needed to seek God more diligently and learn more about Him. This burning, which I refer to as a calling from God, caused Faye and me to take our family to the Assembly of God Church and become members there. We were both baptized in The Holy Spirit as evidenced by speaking in tongues. *"And they were all filled with the Holy Ghost, and began to speak with other tongues, as the Spirit gave them utterance" (Acts 2:4)*

The Lord was doing an excellent work within us at this time. The growth was seemingly unending as we dedicated ourselves to study, prayer, and regular church attendance. I had been having dreams all my life, but when I had approached pastors and other elders, they repeatedly told me to be careful, or I might get involved with something that was not of God. As I grew in knowledge and understanding of the Lord, the dreams started re-occurring. Based on advice from past acquaintances, I became a little concerned, maybe even frightened about having dreams and I began to question if I was on the correct path or not. In my spirit, I knew that God had shown me things from the time I was a young boy, until now, that had to be God. I just knew it inside of me, and the things I was hearing and experiencing were proof of what God had been telling me.

Then something amazing happened, one day, as I was driving home from work. The sun was setting, and the sky was a brilliant red color. I stopped to gaze at the handiwork of God when all of a sudden I saw the sunset turn into a full and beautiful circle. This circle took on the form of a crown. It was glorious in color and splendor. Then I felt a voice in my spirit speaking to me and saying, "Worship the Lord with all your heart, soul and mind. My Splendor and My Glory will be revealed. The vision of the crown is a sign to you that I will use you to minister to the lost. I have ordained it, and I will complete it. Tell the people of My Glory, and speak of this day and the Glory of God which you have seen." With fear and trembling, I shared this vision in our Sunday morning church service. I didn't know if we would be asked to leave or if we would receive affirmation from this congregation. What I knew was this; God had revealed Himself to me, removed the doubt and fear, and confirmed to me what He had been telling me since I was very young. I was so excited that I wanted to quit my job immediately and go on the road proclaiming God's Glory and Goodness. I did not do this. Was I right or wrong to stay in my job? I don't know, and it doesn't matter because God's grace has brought me this far and in writing about these events, I am now proclaiming the Glory and Goodness of God.

Our Pastor and the congregation not only embraced this vision but also encouraged me to continue listening to God for further instructions and guidance. Our Pastor asked me to go with him to Tulsa, Oklahoma to a Prophetic Conference. The pastor of the hosting church in Tulsa had spoken at the Assembly of God Pastors Conference in Alexandria, Minnesota, regarding prophets and the prophetic. He had shared real life experiences about his meeting of the prophets and was encouraging the pastors to learn more about prophets, visitations, and words from God. Pastors and anyone in their congregation who they thought might have the gift of prophecy or call to the prophetic attended the Prophets Conference in Tulsa. Our pastor asked me to go with him since he knew I had many dreams and now experienced an open vision.

We traveled to Tulsa and attended this conference, where we met two prophets of God.
How do I know they were prophets? They met
the requirements! They also chose me out of a
group of about 400 people and told me things
that only God and I could have known. They further gave me prophecies of future events that I
knew I would have to wait for, but that did later
happen. These are very personal things, and
I will not share them here. Over the next few
years, Faye and I regularly attended these con-
ferences in Tulsa. In the fall of 1986, we desired
to attend the Prophetic Conference, scheduled
for late September. We were eager to partici-
pate in this conference, but since I had been
out of work all summer and had only recently
taken a minimum wage job, we did not have the
money to go. Some friends from church offered
us a ride with them, but we still needed money
for the trip. I prayed for $100. Here I will pick up
the dream that I titled THE TRIP.

THE DREAM

In the dream, Faye and I were at the farm of a couple from our church. We were in a long line of people preparing to board vehicles to leave for Tulsa and the Prophetic Conference. As we were standing in line, my Dad came up to me telling me he had something for me. He reached out to hand me an envelope. Faye was closer to him, so she reached to take the envelope and give it to me. Dad pulled it back and said it was for me. I took the envelope but was curious why Faye couldn't accept it. I noticed specifically that the envelope had my name typed on the outside in bold, capital letters. Opening the envelope, I found five $20 bills inside. I was so excited to know that we could attend this conference and that Dad had given us the money. That is when I woke up from the dream.

AFTER THE DREAM

I was somewhat discouraged when I realized that it was a dream. We wanted so much to go to Tulsa. I went about my morning chores, still wondering about the dream. I thought of Mary, the mother of Jesus. *"But Mary kept all these things, and pondered them in her heart" (Luke 2:19).* This scripture best describes the way I felt that morning. It seemed so real that I could not get the events out of my mind.

Later that morning, we received a phone call from our pastor. Faye answered the phone, and our pastor asked to speak to me. He told me that he had an envelope with my name on it. The instructions given by the person who handed it to him, was, to pass the envelope on to me. I drove the twelve miles to the church and met with our pastor. He handed me the envelope that had my name typed on it. He told me that he could not divulge the name of the person who gave it to him. He also said he did not know what the envelope contained. He asked me if I wanted him to stay while I opened it. I said yes; please wait since I do not know what this is. Opening the envelope, I found five $20 bills inside.

I immediately felt goose bumps because that is exactly how it was in the dream right down to the typed name. I was not able to contain my excitement, and I immediately shared the dream with Pastor. He encouraged me to share it in church the next day, which I eagerly did. No one came forward to claim the provision of money. We learned years later that the people who sent us the $100 was the same couple whose farm we were at in the dream when we were preparing to board the vehicles to leave for Tulsa.

APPLICATION OR MEANING

God has every detail covered. If you have what you believe to be a dream from God, pay close attention to the details in the dream. God often gives me dreams of my Dad. In these dreams, my Dad is representative of God. Every detail in this dream had a purpose, and God fulfilled it right down to the letter. His promises are true. *"For verily I say unto you, Till heaven and earth pass, one jot or one tittle shall in no wise pass from the law, till all be fulfilled"* (Matthew 5:18)

Not every dream or vision will come true immediately such as this one did. There are many times when a person has to wait days, months or even years for the fulfillment. Perseverance, patience, and faith are the keys to fulfillment. I have had some dreams that are decades old that have not yet happened, but I have learned from experience that they inevitably will happen, and patience is the key. DO NOT let your dreams go and DO NOT let anyone talk you out of them. You need to hold on to what God has shown you and what God has said to you.

LARGE UNFINISHED BASEMENT

This particular dream was perhaps the second most memorable and influential to me. The first dream that affected my life was the dream of the large house where I walked on the rooftop, and seemed to step upwards from one roofline to the next. I shared that dream earlier in this book.

In this dream, we lived in a rambler style house with a full basement. While surveying the main floor of the house, it was noticeable that it was not extremely large-perhaps about 1200 square feet. I made my way to the basement, and at first, I felt sick from what I found. I found piles and piles of dirt, some as high as six feet, with trampled, and packed down dirt paths around the piles.

As I came around one pile of dirt, I found my Dad laying twelve-inch square tiles on the dirt piles. He was setting them on the sides of the dirt piles as if finishing the floor. However, the tiles were lying at angles to each other, with large spaces between them, and not fastened down. There was no organization to the method or placement of the tiles. I asked him, "What are you doing? These tiles will not be any good like this. We first have to level and finish the floor then we can add tiles." He said to me, "You just go away, and when you come back, it will be finished." At this point in the conversation, I chose to leave the house. I was thinking what a waste of time and money just to lay tiles on piles of dirt.

When I returned to the house, I went directly to the basement. Everything was amazingly bright, shiny, and clean. The floor was level and had a marble texture that reflected images. The basement was huge; at least 4000 square feet. Looking as far as I could see, the other end of the basement seemed hundreds of feet away. As I walked around, I found that the basement had smooth rounded corners leading to other areas. It was magnificent. There were many furnishings. The furnishings were the kind of furnishings that I would expect to see in a palace. My feelings of joy and gratitude were difficult to express. I had never seen such a beautiful place.

As I awoke from this dream, I spent several minutes just enjoying the euphoria I felt to own such a beautiful house. The most memorable words from the dream were, "You go away, and when you return I will be finished". I immediately knew the meaning of the dream. God was working on the lower parts, the base nature, of my being. There was a magnificent transition occurring within me. God was changing my very nature, my soul, and spirit; from the sinner I had been to the saint that God transitions us into when we become born-again.

I also felt sadness. I thought being told to go away and come back when the work was completed; I would no longer be having any house dreams. After all, this working of God in us takes a lifetime. I so often look forward to going to bed at night so I can experience the dreams. I concluded that the statement "You just go away, and when you come back, it will be finished" meant that I would no longer experience God dreams. That thought could not have been further from the truth. I continue to experience dreams and visions to this day.

APPLICATION OR MEANING

God created the heavens and the earth. *"In the beginning God created the heaven and the earth" (Genesis 1:1)*

God made man (mankind) in His image. *"And God said, Let us make man in our image, after our likeness" (Genesis 1:26)*

That means, from creation, man has the spirit and nature of God within him. Then God gave man boundaries. Boundaries included where and how we should live to enjoy a full and satisfied life. God's intent was for man to live forever.

Man chose differently. The original boundary was the command not to eat of the fruit of the Tree of Life or the Tree of the Knowledge of Good and Evil. Man chose to disobey God, and ate of the fruit of the Tree of the Knowledge of Good and Evil, resulting in a separation from God. Man's spirit and soul are now infected with sin, the result of this disobedience. God called this death. *"But of the tree of the knowledge of good and evil, thou shalt not eat of it: for in the day that thou eatest thereof thou shalt surely die (Genesis 2:17)*

Centuries later, God sent His Son, Jesus, to pay the price for the sin. The penalty, which was eternal separation from God, or death, required payment. This payment required the shedding of blood, without which, there is no remission (forgiveness) of sin. *"And almost all things are by the law purged with blood; and without shedding of blood is no remission"* (Hebrews 9:22). Jesus came from Heaven to Earth to pay that price. He was the perfect sacrifice. He suffered, died on the cross, conquered sin and death, and rose again from the dead. The result of this payment of our sins by Jesus is our forgiveness. Forgiveness comes when we confess our sins and ask Jesus to be our Lord. When we sincerely repent and ask Jesus to be Lord of our life, the devil no longer has a legal right to our soul. He is defeated! If the devil wants to harass and hurt us, he needs permission from God. Jesus' suffering, death, and resurrection satisfied a legal contract that man made with the devil in the Garden of Eden. *"That if thou shalt confess with thy mouth the Lord Jesus, and shalt believe in thine heart that God hath raised him from the dead, thou shalt be saved"* *(Romans 10:9)*

God is willing to take a lifetime to complete the building process in us. We change, that is our spirit changes, when we are born-again; but that is only the beginning. Paul stated, *"Wherefore, my beloved, as ye have always obeyed, not as in my presence only, but now much more in my absence, work out your own salvation with fear and trembling" (Philippi-ans 2:12).* We're told to work out our salvation. God was showing me that the finished product, my soul, and spirit, is a beautiful thing when the work is complete. He sent me away so I would not interfere with what He is doing. This process, of His work within me, is a continuing work. This same work is taking place in each of us. Do not fight against what God is doing, but rather allow Him to finish the work, in His way and His timing. We help ourselves best by knowing when to, and when not to, involve ourselves in what He is doing. Just ask Him, and He will tell you the when, where, how and what you are to do. When we go to Heaven, whether, by death or rapture, our change is complete. This new creature will be beautiful. It is not our work, but the work of God that will make the creature beautiful.

THE ATTIC DREAM 1

In this dream, I found myself in the attic of my dad's house. It didn't resemble any house in which he had lived. This house was enormous and spacious, but we only visited the attic of the house. Looking around the attic, I saw many items, some old, and some new. There were numerous items. More things than I could count. Some things were stacked on top of each other, and some were sitting by themselves. There were many piles, or stacks, of items yet everything was recognizable. Though the attic was dusty, it was not particularly dirty. Most of the items in this space were old, well used and antiques. I also noticed many manikins lying around this vast area, and I could not help but marvel at the quantity of them.

I saw my dad across the attic. He looked old but appeared to be quite agile, though moving very slowly. I watched him as he rummaged through the items as if looking for something in particular. As he moved from place to place, he would often stop to open the lid of a trunk. There were many trunks, filled with an assortment of items, at various locations in the room. Some of these items were clothing, some were knick-knacks, and some were a variety of miscellaneous items and what looked like odds-and-ends. It was plain to see that many, if not all, of the items, were of great personal value to him. He carefully lifted the lid of each trunk, and I watched his face as he viewed the contents. There was an expression of joy and exhilaration on his face as he looked at the treasure inside. He carefully sorted through the items in the trunk handling each with precision and care so as not to damage it. Individual things, not readily identifiable to me, would be set aside as if to be studied or used later.

When dad found certain items, he would call out for my sister Karen. As I continued watching him, he slowly and carefully made his way around the room. Every time he found something that he wanted to share, he would call out to Karen. This process of sorting, saving and calling for Karen continued for quite a long time. Upon waking, I immediately knew what God was telling me in the dream.

APPLICATION OR MEANING

Years ago I sensed in my spirit God telling me to study, teach and restore the old paths. In this dream, God was showing me His store-house, and the many items that are of great value there. As He makes each item avail-able to us, He handles it with great care so as not to damage the item. As He reveals these things, which may be gifts of the Spirit or other treasures of heaven, He calls us by name to receive them. Every time God uses one of my siblings in my dreams, it is representative of a Christian brother or sister. These are gender neutral, sometimes will be one or more of the girls, and sometimes will be one or more of the boys. Each time they appear in a dream, they represent the family of God. God is handing out gifts just as promised in The Scriptures. He selects each gift and personally distributes that gift to the proper recipient. Calling an individuals name shows how much care God places in handing out gifts. We each receive one or more gifts chosen especially for us.

The old and outdated manikins represent people of the past. There were many manikins in the attic, meaning there are many people who have gone before us, from whom we can learn. In Hebrews 11, Paul listed the people of Faith as examples for us. Many of these people are from the Old Testament Scriptures. God did not inspire the writing of the Bible just to pass along a list of rules and regulations. Rather, He had the Bible written as a guidebook, so we could live a life of abundance as we learn from the examples given to us in the book. Many of these manikins, may also represent people we have known. They may be relatives or acquaintances that have influenced our lives in one-way or another. Some may have lived a life of example (either good or bad), and others may have said things, or taught us things, which left a lasting impression on our lives.

I received this dream as encouragement to seek the wisdom of people past, and to seek God for gifts and purposes He may have for us. These gifts and purposes will be used as we walk out our lives in His service here on earth. My prayer for you is that you will also seek God for His gifts and purposes as He calls out your name and distributes the gifts as He wishes.

THE ATTIC DREAM 2

In this dream, I am in the farmhouse where I grew up. My son, Jeremy, and I are walking up the stairs to the second level of the house. We are discussing how my dad left us the house and its contents. At the top of the stairs, down a short hallway is a large bedroom with eastern exposure. As we enter this room, we find many hatboxes and plastic hangers stacked in cubes about the room. Each cube contains four stacks of items. Two of the stacks, each comprised of three hatboxes set on top of each other, stand on opposite corners of the cube. The other two stacks, setting on the opposite corners of the cube from the hatboxes, are plastic hangers stacked on top of each other to a height equal with the hatboxes. The stacks of boxes and hangers inter-changeably make up the cube. Walking around a cube, you would first pass a stack of hangers, and then a stack of boxes, then a stack of hangers, then a stack of boxes. Everything seems ordered neatly with enough space to walk between the cubes. I say to Jeremy, "What will we do with all this stuff"? Not knowing what to do with the stuff, we decide to leave the room and deal with it later.

When we came back later most of the boxes and hangers were gone. The cubes remaining now sit on the north side of the room, occupying only a tiny fraction of the available room space. Now the room appeared much larger than it had previously appeared when there were many cubes in the room. The floor area seemed almost endless. We could now see the floor was blonde hardwood, sparkling, and reflecting light. The room appeared to be its own source of light, emitting a bright white light, such as I had never seen before. I went to an attic door. I turned to Jeremy and told him that there were likely some things in there that Dad left us. There were two doors into the attic. Opening the first door exposed six feet of open space between the first and second doors. The floor in this space had holes, open to the floors below, where the wood had rotted away. We carefully moved to the second set of doors which was two separate doors (pocket doors) sliding in opposite directions. As we opened the pocket doors, we immediately saw numerous antiques in this room. Though this was an attic, there were two or three steps down to get into the attic. I could not understand the steps down; they seemed very peculiar to me.

At the forefront of the attic, sits an enormous sewing machine, measuring six feet wide by four feet high. It is the item most prevalent in the room. It did not escape our attention how much dust covered the other items while this sewing machine is dusted and cleaned. Apparently, all these items have been sitting in there for a long time. Though it also has been in there for a long time, the sewing machine is spotless and polished. The machine's color is a faded purple with gold letters. It's apparent that whoever used it, then stored it, cared a great deal about it. Although it shows some wear on the frame and letters, it still has the appearance of a nearly new machine. The name Singer, in capital letters, and very bold is on the side of the machine.

APPLICATION OR MEANING

The items in the attic are gifts and talents stored up for God's children to use on earth. God is dispersing these gifts and talents to the body of Christ. They have been available since the outpouring of The Holy Spirit on the day of Pentecost, but the body has not received all of them. The attic being down two to three steps signified that the gifts are available to us on earth and are not being stored in some heavenly storehouse where we have to achieve a certain level of goodness, or wait until we get to Heaven, to receive them. The gifts are available for use on earth as we await the return of our Savior. God is not sitting in heaven waiting for us to be good enough or holy enough to receive what He has for us. He is excited about us repenting, being born-again, and receiving the gift of the Holy Spirit, but He gave no requirements for the gifts of the Spirit. They are His to disperse as He wills. There are significant advantages to receiving the gifts as a believer in Christ.

"The husbandman that laboureth must be first partaker of the fruits" (2 Timothy 2:6). *"But in a great house there are not only vessels of gold and of silver, but also of wood and of earth; and some to honour, and some to dishonour"* (2 Timothy 2:20). There are certain gifts reserved for His children, but there are other gifts given to worldly children, used for Godly purposes. An example of this would be a singer. Though they may not know Jesus as their Lord and Savior, many people receive from God a great singing voice, or the talent to play a musical instrument, which they may use to glorify God.

There were two distinguishing factors about the sewing machine. The first was its cleanliness. The cleanliness shows that God is prepared to deliver the gift for use by the person whose time has come. The second distinguishing factor was the word, Singer.

As I was explaining this dream to a friend, I received more of the interpretation. The singer meant that God was calling me to sing, and the gift was ready for delivery. When Jesus ascended to Heaven, He gave gifts to men. *"Wherefore he saith, When he ascended up on high, he led captivity captive, and gave gifts unto men" (Ephesians 4:8).* Dad leaving us the house was symbolic of God handing out gifts. The boxes and hangars represent distractions to finding what gifts God has for you. We had to search to find the attic containing the gifts. You have to search also. There may be many stacks of things distracting you from finding your gift, but keep seeking, and you will find it, or them. The worn out and holey floor represents doubts, and cares of the world, that stop us from seeking God with our whole hearts deep enough to find the gifts. Seek and you will find. Ask God for the gifts He has for you and then let Him develop them in you in the way He desires.

THE LIBRARY

I have included this dream in the building section since it involves a building. This dream is one of the primary dreams that encouraged me to write books.

THE DREAM

I was walking in what I could best describe as an alley, lined with buildings on my right side, and a wire fence on my left side. Beyond the fence was an open field. I approached the back of a uniquely shaped building, having a circular loading dock facing toward me at a forty-five-degree angle from the direction I was walking. I stepped up, onto the loading dock, and made my way to a door. As I entered the building through this door, I immediately recognized it as a library. All along the left and right walls were bookshelves aligned at ninety-degree angles to each other. The bookshelves were about three feet tall with three shelves in each. They created small nooks with a table and four chairs in each nook. There were six nooks on each side of the room. I looked around, and to my amazement, the bookshelves were empty. I wondered how a library could exist with no books. The chairs and tables made me aware that this library was ready for use. All it needs is books.

Walking past the six nooks, I stay in the room as it makes a curve to the right. Rounding the curve, I find myself in a bedroom. There is a king-sized bed with empty bookshelves on both sides of it. The headboard of the bed is also a bookcase with empty shelves. Near the foot of the bed, but about ten feet away, stands a spiral staircase with a black wrought iron rail. I take one step up the staircase only to find a chain across the steps with a metal sign reading "Do Not Enter". I look around and see a man, who says to me, "It is not yet time to go up these steps." I linger in the room for a long time pondering the empty bookshelves, tables, and chairs. Still wondering about the library space and bedroom, I decide to leave the building and come back later. I walk towards the back door and the loading dock, passing the empty book-shelves. I exit the building through the same doors where I entered. Then the dream ended.

APPLICATION OR MEANING

The Lord showed me there are hundreds, even thousands, of books not written, but that people will soon write. Thus, the library shelves remain empty. There are currently many people writing books that others will read and study. These books, will then, occupy spaces on the shelves. God is calling authors to write the material that He has to share with us.

The bedroom represented two things. First, many people are too busy resting and not per-forming the work, especially writing, that God is asking them to do. Secondly, some are not taking the time to rest when they should but are too busy with other things to write the words (books) God has for them to write.

The staircase is symbolic of communication with God. Whatever your work, seeking God's direction and timing, is crucial. God directed me to write, so I set out to write. The writing has sometimes been easy and other times difficult. I attribute the easy times to being in His perfect will. I started writing immediately after this dream, and it was a laborious task. I started writing a book based on what I wanted to write. It failed miserably. God has shown me that I will finish that book, but He has other books more important to get out first. This book has been an easy task under God's direction.

When God gives us a task to perform, that task will be easy if given back to Him, to work it within you. Not every step will be easy, but when finished, you will look back and see how God helped and directed you through the process. The key is to stay in touch with God and wait for

His next direction. The Bible states that if you "Wait on The Lord" He will renew your strength. *"But they that wait upon the Lord shall renew their strength; they shall mount up with wings as eagles; they shall run, and not be weary; and they shall walk, and not faint" (Isaiah 40:31)*

THE ADJUSTMENT

The setting:

Once again, before I share this dream, I am going to set the backdrop for it. I was working as a Quality Technician in the corporate headquarters of an engineering company that had several manufacturing plants across the Midwest part of the United States. As part of my work assignment, I had to travel to these manufacturing plants to calibrate quality control test equipment. The calibration process required me to take along some heavy pieces of equipment that I loaded in the trunk of my car. I had to lift them out of the trunk, place them on carts, and move them around the plant.

I arrived at the first plant the evening before I had to perform their calibration. I was in extreme pain in my lower back that night and was concerned about whether or not I would be able to lift the heavy equipment out of the trunk of the car. I also did not know whether I would be able to perform the work if I needed to use the heavier equipment. As I lay in bed that night, I was praying to God for a miraculous healing in my back. Any movement I made sent what felt like shocks of pain up and down my spine and through my legs. I thought to myself, "Without a miracle, I do not know if I will be able to drive home much less finish my ten-day trip to calibrate equipment at each plant.

THE DREAM

I dreamt I was in the kitchen of a house. I was telling my Dad how much my back hurt. He instructed me to sit on a wooden chair with a very straight back. It had a hard wooden seat and was quite uncomfortable. He told me to sit in the chair with my back as straight as possible. I sat down in as good a posture as I could due to the pain. Dad knelt in front of me, reached out with both hands, and grabbed my hips. With a quick jerking motion, he twisted my hips back and forth then up and down. Feeling immediate relief from the pain, I got up and easily moved around the room. I felt such relief and freedom with the pain totally gone. When I awoke from this dream, I was able to move and work and experienced no more pain for the remainder of the trip.

APPLICATION OR MEANING

"Surely he hath borne our griefs, and carried our sorrows: yet we did esteem him stricken, smitten of God, and afflicted. But he was wounded for our transgressions, he was bruised for our iniquities: the chastisement of our peace was upon him; and with his stripes we are healed" (Isaiah 53:4-5)

"Who his own self bare our sins in his own body on the tree, that we, being dead to sins, should live unto righteousness: by whose stripes ye were healed" (1 Peter 2:24)

When Jesus suffered, died and rose again He carried all our grief (pain, regrets) and sorrow (sadness). By His stripes, we are healed (wholeness in health). So often, we think that we have to go to a special church service, special meeting or to a gifted Evangelist to receive healing from God. The truth is, we have to go to Jesus for our needs. All we need to do is ask, and He will honor His word and fulfill His promise. The work He did and the pain He suffered was not without cause. He is quick to perform His Word if we believe what He says, and if we will ask Him according to His Word. *"And all things, whatsoever ye shall ask in prayer, believing, ye shall receive"* (Matthew 21:22) *"Hitherto have ye asked nothing in my name: ask, and ye shall receive, that your joy may be full"* (John 16:24)

THE PLOW

This dream is a fun dream, but it still has spiritual implications and meaning. The meaning is mostly for me, but you may find it applies to you as well.

THE DREAM

Faye and I walk onto a field where many of my brothers and sisters are busy planting seeds. There are furrows plowed into the ground, and the planters are placing seeds into the furrows. We walk up to where my sister and her husband are planting seeds and start covering the seeds so they would germinate.

My brother-in-law looks up from his work and says to me, "You can't work at this until you have been properly trained and told what to do." Looking around, I see Mom and Dad (who have already gone to Heaven) operating a machine that is plowing the ground and making the furrows. It is a comical sight. The plow is made out of rough and rusty metals, mostly I-Beams. It has framework only, with no panels to hide the metal beams or internal parts of the machine. It has the appearance of the front portion of a grader used in construction. Dad is driving and operating the machine with Mom standing behind him, hanging on as tightly as she can.

The machine is clanging, bouncing side-to-side and forward-and-backward as it performs its task. The clanging sound is relentless as the machine plows the furrows. It appears to bounce upwards, then settle down, and then bounce forward, and then stop and settle backward a little, and then bounce forward again, repeating this over-and-over as it digs the furrow. Dad seems to be exerting all his effort just to keep the machine operating in a straight line. One of the things that stood out in the dream was how he has his legs stretched out nearly in a straight line, parallel to the ground, with his right foot busily operating a foot pedal. The machine has a very low clearance between it and the ground, so Dad's body is in an L shape, bent at the waist about one foot off the ground. It looks very dangerous, but they seem comfortable in its operation.

So here are Mom and Dad, riding on a machine, bouncing up and down, forward and backward, holding on as tight as they can while plowing furrows in a field. What I find really great is how much they seem to be enjoying the work they are doing. Mom is holding on for dear life as her hair blows straight back, caused by the wind and the speed they are moving, which seems strange since they are barely moving forward. Mom is laughing boisterously. I have not seen her enjoying herself and having this much fun for a long time.

We approach the machine to ask what we should do. Dad's attention remains entirely fixed on the machine, and he doesn't even look at us.

Mom is so intent on hanging on that she does not look at us either. All they say is, "You know what to do." So we go over and start covering the seeds in the furrows with soil, to protect the seeds until they germinate. Once we had gone to inquire of Mom and Dad, there were no more questions from anyone regarding what we were doing.

APPLICATION OR MEANING

If you have read previous stories in this book, then you already know that, in dreams, God uses my Dad and my Mom to represent Himself to me. In dreams, He also uses my siblings to represent my brothers and sisters in Christ. This dream is no exception to that rule. The fact that my brother-in-law told me I could not perform the work without special training or special instructions is an important point here. The dream does mean my brother-in-law personally. It is symbolic of people who come into the family of Christ, or into the church, and make judgment

calls about other people's callings and ministries. They make the judgments without the full
understanding of how God works in His family,
how God's calling operates, or what He is doing
in someone's life.

Our going up to Mom and Dad and asking
them about what we should do is symbolic of
our seeking God's gifts and callings for our lives.
Dad, not taking his attention from his work to
talk to us, but only said we know what to do,
was God saying to us, "You know what to do."
In other words, He has told us and instructed
us, as to what our calling is and how we should
move forward with it.

Perhaps you too are struggling with the question of "What does God want me to do in this
life? Or what is my calling?" If you believe you
know what God has called you to do, but you
have doubts regarding that calling due to past
hurts, then ask God. If circumstances have left
you feeling disqualified, I encourage you just to

ask God for clear direction on your calling. Ask Him to heal any wounds or hurts that may cause you to be holding back from fulfilling your calling. He may just tell you that you already know what to do, or He may give you additional information or guidance. If you feel like He is not offering much, it may be because He has already given you direction, and He is just waiting for you to get started. That was our direction. He did not take His attention away from the work. He just made a statement saying that we already know what to do. If that is you, then I say to you, "Go with God's grace. He will direct your paths as you step out in faith to do what is in your heart and spirit to do."

CHAPTER 5

INSTRUCTION AND DISCIPLINE

Not every dream I dream involves my Dad or my Mom. I will now share several dreams God has given me for instruction or discipline. These dreams relate specifically to me. I will also share dreams of instruction or discipline for others. Some of these dreams with their interpretation, as shown in the Application or Meaning section, may benefit you. I ask that you keep an open mind as you read these dreams.

THE MECHANICAL BATTLEFIELD

Setting:

This dream was one of my earliest and most prophetic dreams. I was only nine or ten years old when I had this dream. It left a profound impact on me; I have never gotten over the extreme emotions involved.

THE DREAM

I hear the unmistakable sounds of war as I walk across the field. The recently harvested hay left ankle-high stubble around my feet. Off in the distance, there is a sound of metal rubbing on metal. The sound is the kind of sound you would hear from farm machinery or factory machines in use.

I cross the field and approach a knoll as the sounds become louder and louder. Not knowing what is making the sounds makes me extremely uncomfortable and fearful. Looking over the knoll, I see the source of the sounds. Animal shaped machines moving across the ground, twisting into various shapes, and bending at joints in their bodies are making the sounds. I see alligators, rhinoceros, hippopotamus, elephants, and various other types of animals. As I watch these animal machines fighting and moving, I realize they are not animals at all. They are mechanical beings in the shape of animals fighting a war. The alligator is quite nimble and is the focal point of the battle. It turns its body on hinges and is able to make short turns. The mouth is continually being opened and closed as it swallows the enemy. I find this terrifying and awake in a pool of sweat.

Though this is one of my earliest dreams, I have never shared it with anyone. I was afraid of ridicule and name calling because of what I saw and experienced in the dream. I have never forgotten this particular dream, and it is just as real today as it was when I dreamt it.

APPLICATION OR MEANING

I believe God gave me insight into the future of war. I find the memory and the lesson of this dream fascinating as we learn more and more about drones and their application in today's warfare. We hear of drones in the shape of insects. We hear of people who are part mechanical and part flesh. I have also read about the altering of animals through biotechnology for battlefield use. Could this be how we will fight our next battle?

I understood the meaning of the dream, and I often wondered if I would actually see the day when the battlefield would look like this. I knew that this was a battlefield scenario of the last days but as a child, I never would have guessed that I would see this type of warfare. It seems to be upon us, and I thank God He has chosen to reveal this to me beforehand.

I have shared this dream with other prophets, and other men and women of God. I have received many types of interpretation, including these, "You need to change your diet"; "You take these dreams too seriously"; "I wouldn't be telling people because they will think you are going insane"; "You have unresolved inner conflicts." There are many interpretations or opinions of dreams. If you are having dreams from God, you can be sure that He will make the meaning clear. The interpretation may come through another person, but it will always agree with what God has spoken into your spirit.

I believe God spoke to me in this dream about a coming, end time war, with many mechanical beings doing the fighting. The shapes may not be as I saw them, but filling the battlefield will be mechanical weapons of some sort. I also interpret this dream to say that when I see these things I should know that the return of Jesus is near, and there is a sense of urgency to reach the lost for Christ.

THE LIE

Setting:

It is 4:30 AM. I just awoke from a God dream that I will be adding to my book entitled Heavenly Experiences. Due to the context and message of this dream, I sense an urgency making me share it here immediately.

THE DREAM

A friend and I are riding our motorcycles across the desert. (I know this is a friend, but I never see his face). We are traveling a dirt road that does not appear to have had a significant amount of traffic. As we round a curve, we see a building with a tower type structure next to it. For no apparent reason, we stop near this building.

The tower has cement steps leading to two doors at the top. There are twelve steps, and then a landing, twelve more steps, then another landing at the top, just outside the doors. On the top landing is a pair of orange waders. Through a window in the tower, we see two people inside. We recognize them as guards and realize this is a prison.

As we study this building, two motorcycles stop and join us at the side of the road. We form an immediate bond with these two strangers. They are very friendly and eager to learn about us. We discover they are members of a motor-cycle club, which they would like us to join. This club is not an ordinary biker club but is a recog-nized outlaw club. One of these bikers is the rec-ognized "Leader" of ALL bike riders. Whatever he says, bikers do. (I will refer to him as BL in the rest of this dream).

BL tells us, if we climb this tower and enter it, we can experience the true understanding of being a biker, including the raw emotions con-nected with the brotherhood of this club. We are eager to embrace this feeling of belonging, but knowing this is a prison makes us a little nervous. BL says, "You don't need to be scared, I will go with you." I was still afraid, but agreed to go in as long as BL went with me.

As I prepare to climb the steps, BL gets on his bike. He said he had one quick thing to take care of, but I should go ahead, and he will join me when he returns. I watch him as he slowly rides away. I climb the steps, stopping periodically to look back at my friend and the other biker. They encourage me to keep going. When I get to the top landing, I put on the waders. They were required wear to enter the tower.

I enter the tower through the door on the right. The guards just stand there without looking at me. Inside the door was a short and narrow cement landing. Then the floor took on the shape of an amusement ride. It resembled the track of a roller coaster: the style having only a narrow track, and makes you ride inverted for distances. The track made a 180-degree turn downward and slightly to the left, for about three feet. Then it curved back to the right and resumed a downward path. I could not see the bottom of the track: it went out of sight, under the landing. I knew I was required to grab the track, which would then make me travel face down to the floor below.

There are many mean looking people watching me and cheering me on to grab the track. They are slobbering spit from their mouths and making loud and obnoxious sounds. The door to the left is an exit door, but the guards won't allow me to exit. I think to myself, "When will BL come and rescue me from this situation?" In my confused state, I grab the rail and travel head first to the floor below. My eyes go closed, and I cannot open them. As I pass the people in the crowd, they grab at me, cling to me, and do despicable things to me: I am urinated on, struck in various parts of my body, sexually groped, and crowded so closely, that

I feel incredibly claustrophobic. All this time my eyes are closed, and I cannot open them.

THEN I REALIZE: BL LIED TO ME. There is no escape from this hell. I am stuck in this position: Face down in total darkness, face pushed against the floor, unable to open my eyes, crowded to the point of being claustrophobic with beings attacking me, FOR ALL OF ETERNITY! Then I awoke.

APPLICATION OR MEANING

No biker should be offended regarding the bikes or bikers in this dream. God used these symbols because I could relate to them.

The bikes represent freedom and independence. We ride the bikes down dirt paths representing our desire for non-conformance to what others might call normal. Some people might even call it rebellion.

My biker friend represents people who claim to be our friend but will either leave and neglect us or turn on us when times of temptation come. BL represents the enemy of our souls, the devil. BL lied to me to get me to enter the tower. He said it would give me a better understanding of life and biking. He assured me that he would be there so I could get back out of the tower, but he didn't come back. It was a trap, and I fell into it with all my being.

The devil works like that. He makes promises, lures us into situations that are harmful, even fatal, to us. Some of the lies he tells us seem plausible, even pleasurable. He doesn't even have to stay around to see the completion of what he has started. Once he tempts us to sin, he can leave. Our hearts and minds will often take over what he has started, and lead us into sin. The temptation isn't the sin; acting on the temptation is the sin.

We need to read The Bible and do as it says. Jesus says that His sheep will know His voice. We have to stay in touch with Him, God, through His Word (The Bible) to know His voice.

This dream is a warning to all of us. Do not be taken in by promises of knowledge, pleasure, fame, etc. Let God do the leading. As satisfying as this world's pleasures seem, they end in death and destruction. "For what is a man profited, if he shall gain the whole world, and lose his own soul? or what shall a man give in exchange for his soul?" (Matthew 16:26)

CHAPTER 6

HIGHWAY DREAMS

"Because strait is the gate, and narrow is the way, which leadeth unto life, and few there be that find it" (Matthew 7:14)

THE RIBBON HIGHWAY

I am in a car with my Dad going on a road trip. We have reached the Canadian border where we will cross into Canada. Dad is telling me that part of the trip involves driving "The Ribbon Highway." The Ribbon Highway passes through several small towns where we have to decrease our speed. Dad states that further on I can take a new highway that bypasses many of the towns. I notice The Ribbon Highway is a narrow, two-lane road that disappears into the heavens. It is a curving road with many small inclines and rises. Along both sides of the road, grow bright colored flowers. Their aroma is sweet and refreshing. It seems vital in the dream to take particular notice of the highway. The asphalt is pitch black, shiny, and new.

Before we can get onto The Ribbon Highway, we have to cross a patrolled border. We stop the car and walk to the crossing gate, where the guard asks to see my ID. I say I must have left it in the car. To return to the car for the ID requires me to cross a very wide schism. There is a platform on which to cross the schism, but to reach the platform I have to descend a steep thirty-foot cement wall. The cement wall has one-half inch square re-bar sticking out of the cement about three inches. These re-bar are all that is available for footing and handholds. I start down the wall, stopping about ten feet off the ground, where the platform crossed the schism. The platform is still three feet away from where I stand on the re-bar. The only way to reach the platform is to swing outward with one hand from a nearby piece of re-bar. To reach the nearby piece of re-bar I have to jump, grab the re-bar and swing across to the platform. I'm not sure I can reach the re-bar, or if I do reach it, I'm not sure I will be able to swing myself far enough, to get to the platform. Looking down at the ten-foot gap between the ground and me, I feel stranded on the small rebar while trying to get a hand-hold to swing out to the platform. I am terrified; nearly paralyzed with fear. I don't know what to do! That's where I woke up; in such terror that I felt like my heart might stop.

APPLICATION OR MEANING

I'm not sure I have the full interpretation of this dream, but I know and believe it signifies that God has a path for each of us to follow. In the dream, The Ribbon Highway represents our walk with Christ.

The schism, or crossing, represents life's challenges. It would seem as though I have come to this crossing unprepared, much like Jesus said about the wedding guests who did not have wedding clothes on. *"And when the king came in to see the guests, he saw there a man which had not on a wedding garment: And he saith unto him, Friend, how camest thou in hither not having a wedding garment? And he was speechless: Then said the king to the servants, Bind him hand and foot, and take him away, and cast him into outer darkness, there shall be weeping and gnashing of teeth" (Matthew 22:11-13)*

While trying to go back to get the ID, or garments, required for the wedding (spending eternity in Heaven), I have taken the wrong route and ended up in a dangerous place. I am at a schism, but I don't know exactly how to get across. The Ribbon Highway seems to represent our salvation journey. Often we take the wrong route to get to Jesus. We try to gain salvation by doing good works; we try religious rituals or other means to seek God. Jesus said that He is the way, the truth, and the light. *"Jesus saith unto him, I am the way, the truth, and the life: no man cometh unto the Father, but by me" (John 14:6).* The path to salvation is not difficult. If we are struggling under a heavy load to find Jesus or salvation, then we need to understand this; all we need to do is ask for forgiveness, and ask Jesus to be our Lord. The crossing is the point where we come to a personal relationship with Jesus Christ.

The Bible describes The Ribbon Highway. *"But small is the gate and narrow the road that leads to life, and only a few find it"* (Matthew 7:14). This highway is our Christian Journey. We have to walk it out, but as we grow and become more like Christ, we can bypass many of the smaller towns or obstacles that would slow us down. Many Christians ahead of us have had to slow down and walk through these towns, but thanks to their efforts we can go around some of these places. The towns are representative of times of learning or hard times. If we heed the words of the Bible and the words of mature, and perhaps more experienced Christians, we can avoid some of these issues (towns).

I struggled with the ID until The Holy Spirit reminded me that when we are born-again we get a new identity, and we no longer have our old identity. *"Therefore, if anyone is in Christ, he is a new creation; the old has gone, the new has come" (2 Corinthians 5:17).* If we try to go back, or if we return to the former lifestyle of sin, we will end up in a dangerous place (the schism). We need to take our new identity and walk The Ribbon Highway. It will lead us to the Promised Land.

While researching the ribbon highway on the Internet, I learned about a highway called THE RIBBON HIGHWAY. It runs from California to Washington and is written about and described in three books. Reading these books, I learned the ribbon highway goes through many small towns, has many hills, and is very crooked. God often uses images or objects from this world to teach us spiritual principles or lessons. Always be open to what God may be showing you. The Ribbon Highway in this dream was symbolic of the narrow path. It is a good and clean highway, but the path is narrow and the banks are steep. We cannot see what is around each curve or bend in the road as we walk out our salvation, but if we trust God, He will make a safe way for us. The path is inclined since it leads to heaven. I pray that your walk on The Ribbon Highway is safe and fruitful.

THE BUSY HIGHWAY

I recently had another short dream involving a highway. This highway has ten lanes in one direction. The two lanes on the far right are exiting lanes and are bumper to bumper with slow and even sometimes stopped traffic. Each lane that is further to the left is a lane for faster-moving vehicles. The highway is very busy with cars in all lanes. The cars in the far left lane are traveling at the fastest speed and seem to be able to continue at a high rate of speed with no hold-ups or slowing.

I am in a car in the far right lane that is moving very slowly. We often stop for cars from the third lane to make their way into the second lane. Each driver in the second lane readily allows the drivers from the third lane to enter the second lane. Some drivers from the second lane would move to the first lane. Nobody in the first or second lane seems impatient or competitive. Each driver is willing to let people in from the third lane. Some drivers from the fourth and fifth lanes are making their way over to the exit lanes as well. Again, drivers willingly let them enter and not seem impatient or in a hurry thus stopping the drivers from moving to the right lanes. There are only two lanes exiting, so traffic slows to allow these drivers into the two right exiting lanes. I notice that ahead of us the two right lanes make a steep incline, curve to the left, and disappear into the sky. I immediately recognize this as the narrow road to heaven, and the cars exiting the highway are going to heaven.

APPLICATION OR MEANING

The drivers and cars represent people traveling through this life. Many are in a hurry, symbolized by the far left lane, and miss all preparation for eternity. The two right lanes are symbolic of the narrow highway to Heaven. The cars and drivers exiting into these lanes have made Jesus the Lord of their lives and found salvation.

As people enter the Kingdom (the narrow road), we have to be patient with them. Many do not understand what has happened and what the expectations are. The exit lanes provide ample room for anyone desiring to enter. It is our responsibility to allow them in and not to try and "cut them off" from entering the Kingdom of God as represented by the exiting lanes in this dream.

ROMEO

This particular dream was not a highway or house dream, yet it contains elements of both.

THE DREAM

Several of my siblings and I are sitting and talking in a room that appears to be under-ground, and yet is not. It is a mound shape or dome-shaped room. There are many things in the room, which makes me think someone lives there. The only entrance and exit is a hatch type door at the top of the room, or dome, with a ladder positioned so we can climb to the hatch (door).

As we're visiting, a man in a white robe walks into the room. He walks up to me and says, "Hello. My name is Romeo. I come from the throne room of God, and I have a message for you". As soon as he says this, we hear a police siren outside. I rush up the ladder to the door to see what is happening. As I reach the door, I see a police car drive by, with red lights flashing and siren whaling. I come back down the ladder and sit down.

The angel approaches me again and says, "Hello. My name is Romeo. I come from the throne room of God, and I have a message for you". As soon as he says this, we again hear a siren outside. I run up the ladder to the door to see what is happening. As I reach the door, I see a fire truck drive by, with red lights flashing and siren whaling. I come back down the ladder and sit down.

Then Romeo says to me for the third time, "Hello. My name is Romeo. I come from the throne room of God, and I have a message for you". As before, as soon as he said this to me we heard another siren outside. I ran up the ladder to the door to see what is happening. As I reach the door, I see a police car and a fire truck drive by, with red lights flashing and siren whaling. I come back down the ladder and sit down. Then I awoke from the dream. As I am waking up, I am upset at myself for not listening to what the message from God was.

I shared this dream with my Pastor, who said to me, "I believe I would get some time alone with God." I went home and asked God what the dream meant. Isn't it amazing how all we have to do is ask? A well-known pastor and sought after speaker at a church in Tulsa, Oklahoma said to us during a Prophetic Conference, "If you do not know the meaning of the vision or the dream, ask God. He will tell you the interpretation". Following his advice, that is what I did. When I asked God for the interpretation, I immediately received, in my spirit, this interpretation, and word from the Lord:

The dream is the interpretation. The emergency vehicles symbolize how I view life's events. The angel came, to give me a word from God, and I chose to place my attention on the things of this world, things that seemed to be emergencies to me. At this time in our lives, I had been out of work for months. Finances were tight and every month brought a new round of challenge to pay the bills and put groceries on the table. My whole life's attention revolved around money. The Lord was showing me that the cares of life were choking out the Word of God. *"And the cares of this world, and the deceitfulness of riches, and the lusts of other things entering in, choke the word, and it becometh unfruitful"* (Mark 4:19)

APPLICATION OR MEANING

"Take my yoke upon you, and learn of me; for I am meek and lowly in heart: and ye shall find rest unto your souls" (Matthew 11:29). Any-thing we face can be an emergency or crisis if we let it. This world is full of distractions from God. We must keep our focus on God and not let the emergencies of life steal messages from God or steal God's word from us. He has things for us to learn, and we have not always been giving Him the

time required to learn them. The message was this: Listen to Me and learn from Me. *"No man can serve two masters: for either he will hate the one, and love the other; or else he will hold to the one, and despise the other. Ye cannot serve God and mammon" (Matthew 6:24).* We cannot serve both God and money. I wish I could say that ever since I dreamt this dream and received its interpretation, I have not worried or neglected the Word due to "emergencies" of this world. I am growing in this, and I pray you will also grow in this. *"But seek ye first the kingdom of God, and his righteousness; and all these things shall be added unto you" (Matthew 6:33).*

Perhaps you also are in a season of cares. Are the cares of this world choking out the Word of The Lord? God wants first place in our lives. Only then can we live a life of peace and abundance as He promised. *"The thief cometh not, but for to steal, and to kill, and to destroy: I am come that they might have life, and that they might have it more abundantly" (John 10:10).*

CHAPTER 7

MACHINERY

Machinery in dreams usually represents trials, hardships, or warnings of danger ahead. I have many dreams about machinery. Some dreams are more specific than others. I will share a generic type dream with its meaning and then I will share one specific dream I had very recently with its meaning.

GENERIC MACHINERY DREAMS

I find myself often dreaming about working in a factory or working around factory machines. In most of these dreams, I have somehow gotten into the spaces around the machines and am in danger of the machines catching, hitting, or pulling me into them thereby hurting or killing me.

APPLICATION OR MEANING

When I have these types of dreams, I can usually relate back to some stress that I am going through at the time. I do not call all of these dreams heaven-sent dreams but rather most are stress-induced dreams. I can usually relate the dream to a situation in my life where I feel trapped or feel extreme anxiety.

Perhaps you have similar dreams where you feel you are in danger or pressure. It may not be machinery in your dreams; it could be animals, storms, or people. If you do have these types of dreams, I recommend that you take the time to analyze where you are in life and what is happening around you. If something is causing great stress, or if you recognize certain areas of danger in your life, then I suggest you seek God for an answer to those situations. God is faithful and will always make a way of escape.

There is one machine dream that I know was from God. I have titled it Battleships, and I will share it on the following pages.

BATTLESHIPS

There are two of us in this dream standing on a hill overlooking a large valley. I know, instinctively, that we are in North Dakota. Directly in front of us, and throughout the valley ahead of us, are huge pieces of equipment: mills, lathes, punch presses, and other factory machines. We are preparing these machines for operation in making parts and assemblies. The tops of these machines stand very high, requiring us to look skyward to see them. All we can see of the machines in the valley are the very tops of them. They resemble the tops of skyscrapers or high mountain peaks. As I gaze at the machines, I am wondering how I am going to operate them since I am unfamiliar with them.

We are standing in front of the closest row of large machines. These machines are anchored in cement and setting on the bank of a hillside that descends into a valley in front of us. Although the row of machines directly in front of us blocked our view of the valley, we were able to see the very tops of the machines that sat in the valley. There is very little space between the machines in this front row. To get to the machines in the valley, we have to turn sideways and push our way forward between the machines.

As we begin to squeeze sideways between two machines, I notice one of the machines moving out of the valley and coming past us just to our right. It was then that I recognized it as a battleship. Pressing through between the front rows of machines, I can now see into the valley. Cement platforms, which anchored the machines, are all I see. Every machine has departed from the valley. I suddenly understand that these machines are not machines at all. They are all battleships, and they have left the valley and sailed. Then the dream ended.

APPLICATION OR MEANING

At the time of this writing, I am still seeking God about this dream. The battleships could represent the oil platforms of North Dakota relocating; meaning the oil industry of North Dakota is nearing an end. The other possible meaning of the dream is that we are about to enter a time of warfare over oil. These are only potential interpretations as of this printing. Neither of these interpretations is pleasant. I am still seeking God regarding the entire interpretation.

CHAPTER 8

DREAMS OF DIRECTION

I received the dreams in this section, but they are directional for other individuals. When I receive a dream of direction for someone else, I always seek God for the timing of sharing that dream with the person. Many people have thanked me for sharing dreams while others have been offended or have brushed them off as nonsense. Many times dreams can apply to multiple individuals since many people have similar experiences in life. We know that we all wear clothes, we all eat food, we all need finances, and we all go through good times and bad times. These life events qualify us to have similar events in life and many of the same needs from God.

As you read these dreams and their applications, you may find they relate to you. If they do relate to you, that does not mean that I have some extraordinary view into your life. What it may mean is that you have similar needs as someone else has, and God has used this media to speak to you. Perhaps, many people can relate to the dream.

THE TITHE

Setting:

A series of job promotions landed me a position of Quality Manager at a factory in Minnesota. As part of the management team, I was privy to information not shared with every employee, and I had easy access to the owners. Some of that information involved the financial status of the company. This company had been very profitable but had fallen on hard times due to the state of the economy. It was not the fault of any one person or department. It was just how the economy was at this time. I spent a great deal of time praying for this company. I was praying for the company and my family since this was our primary source of income. I did not look forward to seeking new employment in that economy. God, always knowing our needs, answered my prayers for this company with this dream.

THE DREAM

In this dream, my dad approaches me and says, "If the owners of this company will tithe off their net profit, the company will not fail but will prosper." That was the end of the dream.

Not wanting to change my mind about sharing this dream, I decided to pass it along as quickly as possible. With fear and trembling, I went to the owner's office the next day. I shared the dream with the senior partner of the company who told me that he would gladly give a tithe except his partners would not approve of such a thing. I left his office feeling sorrowful, not because he did not respond favorably to the dream, but because I knew that if they did not tithe, the company was in jeopardy of financial ruin. That was, after all, their current financial position. However, God was offering them a solution to their financial dilemma. I never heard if they tithed or not. I can only suppose that they did not because one year later, the companies assets were sold, and everyone who worked there, lost their job.

APPLICATION OR MEANING

God is looking for obedience to His word. He is gracious and forgiving, that is a fact, but He is also seeking faith from His children. It takes faith to be obedient to God. Tithing is both an Old Testament and a New Testament teaching although Old Testament laws required payment of a tithe. The New Testament mentions the tithe, but it is not in a context of law. Jesus stated that people should tithe, but not forget good works. *"Woe unto you, scribes and Pharisees, hypocrites! for ye pay tithe of mint and anise and cummin, and have omitted the weightier matters of the law, judgment, mercy, and faith: these ought ye to have done, and not to leave the other undone" (Matthew 23:23)*

When God gives us direction to do something we need to be obedient to perform it. That does not mean, that every time someone says he or she has a word for us, we have to obey it. That word given should align with what God has already been speaking to us, and it will always align with the Word of God. If the word given does not fit, or align, with what is happening in our lives, then we should just shelve it. It is possible that the words shared, may aid, or give understanding into future events. Then you will know it was from God, and you may already have some insight into what the meaning is or how to handle a situation. These messages can be very emotional and need to be presented to The Lord in prayer to determine if they are truly God's will for your life. Many a life has suffered tears and sadness because some well-meaning Christian has spoken a word to someone, and that word was not from God. Seek God on ALL matters.

THE SPANKING

In this dream, I have an overhead view of a boxing ring. There is a gigantic, ugly, mean ogre in the ring. He is holding a baby across his lap and spanking the baby over-and-over-and-over. The poor baby's behind is blistered and red, and he's gasping for breath from crying so hard, that I wonder if he will die. The ogre continues to spank him in spite of the crying and wailing. I recognize this baby as our son. Anger rises within me, and I start toward the ring. I don't care how big this being is; I am going to kill him. Then the baby turns and looks at me. The face suddenly becomes my face, and I realize that I am the one receiving the spanking. I woke up and immediately understood the meaning of the dream.

APPLICATION OR MEANING

The ogre represented Satan. There is no question about that. This dream revealed the devil was hurting me and hurting me a lot. The dream was instructional, telling me I needed to get angry at the devil and learn how to stop him from hurting me. We stop the devil by exercising our authority in Christ. I made it a mission to learn more about this authority. Some excellent books are written explaining this. The best books are Matthew, Mark, Luke, and John.

The devil has no authority over a child of God. He will try to make us think that we are at his mercy, but that is a lie. If he can make us believe the lie, then he can hurt us and make our life miserable. Exercise your authority in Christ and stand against the devil and he will flee from you. *"Submit yourselves therefore to God. Resist the devil, and he will flee from you" (James 4:7).* If the devil is beating you up, then I implore you to learn about your authority in Christ. *"Ye are of God, little children, and have overcome them: because greater is he that is in you, than he that is in the world" (1John 4:4)*

THE REJECTION

Setting:

I have spent a great deal of my life backslidden. At the age of nine, God called me to minister His Word to the lost and hurting of the world, but I had trouble staying on course. I spent much of my life seeking God only to fall away again. At the age of twenty-nine, I gave my heart to the Lord for the very last time. What I mean by that is: I would follow Jesus from that day forward and not let anything stand in my way of serving Him.

Within one week of that experience, I had a dream about a fellow worker. I will call him Henry though that is not his real name. Henry is an engineer by trade, Harley-Davidson bike rider, dedicated father, and an all around very nice person. If you did not know him, his long hair, tattoos, and leather apparel might make you think he was a dangerous person. Henry was not dangerous. In fact, he was a devoted family man, who stood for principle, but was patient and kind. Henry and I became good friends at work.

THE DREAM

Henry and I are standing before God on Judgment Day. Henry is being thrown out of heaven while I am being invited in. (Matt 22:13) Henry looks at me with a lost look, and says to me, with tears in his eyes, "You never told me." I woke up in distress and near panic over the message I had received. I wasted no time in telling Henry about Jesus. The next time I saw him, I shared the story of Jesus and God's great plan of salvation for all.

APPLICATION OR MEANING

God calls every one of us to go forth and preach the Gospel. *"And he said unto them, Go ye into all the world, and preach the gospel to every creature" (Mark 16:15).* If you cannot go to other nations, we have plenty of neighbors right at home that need to hear the Good News of Jesus Christ. We also have many missionaries that need our love and support as they sacrifice their time and life to travel to other countries to preach the Gospel.

Follow-up:

Talk about a wake-up call. I made it my mission in life to tell as many people as I could about The Gospel of Jesus Christ. I hurt way deep down inside from the realization that I did not share the gospel with this man. I was sad for him and angry with myself. I woke up feeling sick to my stomach knowing this man, who was so kind and gentle, was turned away from heaven, when I had the opportunity to share the Gospel with him but did not do so. I approached Henry the next day at work and shared the plan of God's salvation with him. He thanked me for caring but did not commit to making a decision for Christ. I pray he has or will make that decision. As for me, my life's mission is sharing the Gospel with as many people as I can.

THE DEPOT

Setting:

I am sharing this dream exactly the way I presented it to my son, Jeremy.

THE DREAM

Jeremy, my Mom, and my brothers Arlen, Larry, and I are sitting at a table in the depot of an old railroad station, or some call it a yard. Looking outside, I see burned boards on the water tower, and various signs in the railroad yard melted. The entire yard is the type you would see from the old railroad days when steam locomotives traveled the rails. The main building, or depot, is a small wooden structure with dual doors on each end. Inside are wooden benches where people wait for the arrivals and departures of the trains. A wooden platform extends across each end of the building allowing travelers to step off and onto the train from the platform. There is a ticket station inside the depot with a window to the outside as well as to the inside.

My dad (Grandpa Stuber) is standing next to you. Larry had left the room, but the rest of us are still there. Dad (Grandpa Stuber) is saying to you, "You are the one who will take over. You will meet the train. Your brothers will help you. While Larry was in the basement, he said that he would give you his support. You are the one to meet the train and take over this station." All my brothers nodded their heads in agreement that they would help and support you as you take over the station.

On the north side of the yard stands an old building that is in disrepair and starting to collapse. There's a set of railroad tracks running alongside that building. However, they are no longer in use. The newer train tracks, the ones currently being used, lay along the east side of the depot then curve and continue along the north side as well. Though we cannot see it, somehow we know the train will have to go over a bridge that is shaky, missing supports and appears to be nearly collapsing.

Then we hear the train whistle. You leave the depot and go to the north side of the collapsing building to meet the train. Somehow, I know this is the wrong location and that you are supposed to meet the train when it stops on the east side of the depot. Then the train came into the train yard, but it came on a track that was between the depot and the collapsing building. You are over beyond the falling building by the old tracks and not in a location to meet the train. I am desperately trying to get your attention so you can come and meet the train. Somehow, I know that the person who will confirm your taking over is on the train. There is a sense of urgency for you to meet the train. The person you are to meet does not know you. That person only knows that whoever meets the train first is the person who will take over the depot. I don't want the wrong person in the depot to meet the person on the train. If this happens, then the wrong person will be in charge of the depot (church). As I'm trying to wave to you to get you to come back to the depot, you stop at a railroad car on the east side of the falling building. This car was not part of the train that just arrived but was a car that had been previously sitting there. You try to get the car door open, but no matter how hard you try the door will not budge. There is nothing in that car, but you don't know that. You think this car is from the train that has just arrived.

The scene changes:

You are now standing next to the car on the east side of the depot. The train that had just arrived has disconnected this car, left it on the east side of the main depot, and left the train station. Passengers fill the car where you stand. Somehow, I know this is your congregation that you are to take over, but once again, you are unable to open the door and release the people from inside the car. We soon learn that everyone inside this railroad car is sick with MRSA (highly contagious and very deadly). The passengers' condition does not seem to bother you at all. You get the door open and proceed to minister to the needs of every person without concern for your own safety or health.

The scene jumped ahead again. (This portion was as if we were watching a movie). The people are filing into the depot in a single file line. We are watching as you direct them to seats and cots, helping each of them with great love and gentleness. Some need special personal care while others receive help in groups. Then I awoke.

APPLICATION OR MEANING

I knew the meaning of most of the dream and its symbolism. However, I asked God about the train car and why the door would not open. He said to me, "Jeremy will know the answer." Just share the dream with him this morning.

When I shared the dream, Jeremy knew it's meaning as well. He shared with me that God had revealed this to him through another group of individuals. Through this dream and the other group, God was showing Jeremy that he would be taking over a congregation, or perhaps more than one congregation, that had become sick. The sticking door represents churches that may not think Jeremy qualified for what God has chosen him to perform, and, therefore, some resistance occurs. The sickness was doubt, unbelief, gossiping, backstabbing, etc. These sins are extremely contagious, and the sin can spread like wildfire in a congregation. As of this printing, Jeremy has experienced one such congregation. Just like in the dream, we watched as he ministered healing and spiritual guidance to many people. Some received his ministry while others dismissed his efforts and some even rejected him. Jeremy revealed and manifested God's grace as he patiently and kindly went about God's work with this group of people. We are praying for him as God shows him his next work.

Many people receive the call from God to minister to the hurting. You may have received this call, and then been told by a church, or churches, that you are not qualified. Ask God about your mission. He will reveal to you how to perform your calling. Your work may not be the same as Jeremy's work, but trust God and He will show you what and how to perform it.

THE HOTEL

The dream as I told it to my sister Diane:

Faye and I are trying to sleep in the over-sized lobby of an old hotel. The building is five stories tall with wide staircases leading from one floor to the next. Every board and wall in the building needs paint. Cobwebs hang from every doorway. The halls and rooms are ornate, but everything, including all the furniture, is old, dusty and falling apart. I am tossing and turning the entire night as my thoughts revolve around how this place could very well be full of bugs, spiders, and bats that might crawl on us in the night. The bed feels dirty and extremely uncomfortable. I wonder why we chose to be in such a dirty, empty, cold place.

I awoke, but I was only awake in the dream. I start to get out of bed and as I do the lobby of this old hotel starts turning into the most beautiful hotel lobby I have ever seen. I have been in the lobby of the Plaza in NY, and as elegant as it is, it does not compare to the beautiful transformation happening right before my eyes.

Looking down the stairway, near the bottom of the steps, I see two strollers. They lay folded like they are ready for storage, but they are blocking the steps, preventing anyone from using the stairs. Together, lying end to end, they do not reach all the way across the width of the steps, so something fills the space between them. I cannot determine what that is. The purpose of the strollers is very clear. The strollers, set in that position, keep everybody coming out of their hotel rooms, from entering the lobby. At first, I wonder why anyone would be staying in such a dirty dumpy place. Then I realize, we are here, although I am not sure why. I look again at the stairway, and as I follow it upwards with my eyes, it transforms right before me into a palace-style, broad stairway, carpeted with the most beautiful carpeting I have ever seen. I look around the lobby again, and as I place my eyes on certain items, they become new, bright, and very gorgeous. I think to myself, only Heaven can compare to the beauty I am seeing! There are pillars of marble, many of which hold full-length mirrors. The entire lobby transforms into a magnificent hotel lobby almost beyond description. The wood is cedar and reminiscent of a Victorian style mansion. As the stairway transforms, the strollers disappear.

Walking up the open stairway, I notice a room at the top with the door open. Looking in, I see a room about 30 feet wide by 40 feet long. At first glance, I see dirt and disrepair throughout the room. Then I notice a bed with someone in it; someone is tossing and turning just as I had been doing in the lobby bed. I recognize the person in the bed as my sister Diane. As she rolls over and gets out of bed, the room transforms into an elegant bedroom, with canopied bed and beautiful bed linens. The molding along the ceiling becomes new, and I can see that it is hand carved and of exquisite design. The entire room becomes bright and cheerful. To see the transfiguration is like viewing a rustic cabin becoming a royal castle.

As the scene shifts, I once again find myself in the lobby of the hotel. Looking down the hallway, away from the lobby, I can see doorways to other rooms start to brighten as light and sparkles come forth from the room. I sense in the next room, there is an awakening taking place but I am not sure who is in there. For some reason I thought it was my son Jeremy, but it did not look like him.

Then the scene shifts again, and I find myself on the outside of the building. I was on a rickety walkway that went around the entire outside of the building. Observing the hotel from the outside, I can see it has many levels. The walkway followed along many contours, both horizontal and vertical. Parts of the walkway are like new, and other parts are worn and ready to collapse. We carefully walk along the rickety boardwalk examining the outside of the building.

Strolling along directly in front of me, and sometimes at my side, is my Mom. She is securing the walkway as she and I walk along. Parts of the walkway are pulling away from the building, but Mom just pushes it back against the building and says, " This will need to be repaired"! Rounding a corner of the building, I encounter a spot so badly damaged that I cannot make it any further. I say to Mom, "I cannot make it along the walkway because I will fall." Mom just looks at me, holds the walkway up to the building, and says, "This will need to be repaired"! Walking further along the walkway, a friend of Diane's comes around a corner of the building, carrying a handful of weeds. His face is so bright and smiley, and he looks so happy and proud as he exclaims, "I got some more weeds!" The dream ends at this walkway.

APPLICATION OR MEANING

The old building and its size represent the works and efforts of our life. Awakening from our sin and entering into a life of repentance, worship, and service to Jesus, our lives become full of beauty. The transformation of the building, into a building of great size and beauty, with marble and magnificence, is representative of what God is doing in our lives as we surrender to God's Grace and Love. This transformation happens to each of us. Since by now we know that my siblings represent my brothers and sisters in Christ, we can say this is true for all of God's children. If we allow God to take our life and use it to His glory, He will turn it into a thing of beauty.

Mom represents God in the dream as He leads us on our path through this life. The pathway is the journey through this world. The path gets rickety due to our choices and due to circumstances of life. God will keep us safe on our life's journey. He will also direct us by telling us where our lives "need repair", or stated another way, "where our lives need transforming by The Holy Spirit." The weeds are symbolic of

the things of this world that seem to be useless, but God will use the seemingly useless to
change us into something beautiful and useful.
That is why when the weeds, or troubles, come
we are thankful and happy because then God
is going to do something beautiful in our life.
Sometimes even our friends will be the ones
who bring sorrow, or weeds, into our life. Thank
them for it.

CHAPTER 9

A SELECTION OF ASSORTED DREAMS

I n this section, I have assembled a group of eclectic dreams. They don't necessarily fit under any direct type or heading, but each dream has meaning and application.

THE KEYS

Setting:

This dream took place while I was working toward my ministerial license. God had taken us to a small town where I studied for the ministry under the pastor. It was a tumultuous time for us again financially, and I was doing my best to stay on top of bills, study, and give as much time as I could to ministry work. I was beginning to doubt my calling into the ministry and feeling sad because I did not know what else I would do. My job, my occupation, no longer seemed interesting to me, and the ministry seemed elusive at best. Then I had this dream. It was very short and plain.

THE DREAM

I am talking to our pastor when he suddenly hands me the keys to the church building. That was it. It left me wondering what it exactly meant. He was a church planter so I assumed he was going to start a new church, and I would be in charge of this church.

APPLICATION OR MEANING

My interpretation could not have been further from the truth. It was a few years later that the meaning came to me. I had made application to a fellowship to receive my ministry credentials. Part of that process involved a recommendation from my pastor. He readily gave me the recommendation, which caused me to gain approval for licensing. I was later ordained with this fellowship and remain so to this day. This pastor also started a Bible school. Faye and I attended, and graduated from this school. A few years later, we administrated the school. The recommendation, the schooling, and the opportunity to serve in the church allowed me to get my credentials. Therefore, I can say that he indeed handed me keys. They were keys to the ministry and not keys to the building.

E-1

I am still waiting for the meaning, or interpretation, of this dream. Therefore, the application or meaning will be different from the application or meaning of other dreams.

THE DREAM

Several people I know are standing with me on a balcony of a tall office building. The building is gorgeous with the external surface made of blue glass, the kind that reflects the light from the outside but when standing inside, looking out, looks like regular glass. There are several supervisors, who happen to be priests, on the balcony. They are handing out work assignments. One of my fellow workers is standing next to me. A supervisor, or priest, hands her a stapler saying she and I had to share it. I am upset that I cannot have my own stapler. Since other people have their own staplers, it makes me feel like I am less important. This fellow worker in the dream is a close acquaintance in our life.

Then the priest tells me to report to office E-1. I go down to the lowest level, which is an exact replica of an office in a gorgeous office building where I once worked. I am elated that I get to have an office in this place. The office overlooks a large and beautiful lobby area of the building. There are other individual offices around the lobby. One person works from each office, although it is large enough for four. The office's furnishings are exquisite, and the work environment is inviting. That is the end of the dream. I received no work direction or knowledge of what my new job was, only that E-1 is now my office. For some reason having this office makes me extremely happy and proud.

APPLICATION OR MEANING

I am still waiting for the meaning to this dream. I know E-1 is crucial. I have researched

E-1 and found that there is an area in Israel called E1. I do not know if that has anything to do with the dream or not, but I know God will reveal His purpose in the fullness of time.

I write this to encourage you. You might have dreams where you are waiting for the interpretation. Just trust God. In due season, He will reveal it and bring it to pass.

DESSERT TIME

I am not sharing each dream I have dreamt with desserts as the theme, but I am sharing the general concept. I had several dreams regarding church socials and lunches held at a church we attended.

In these dreams, we gather for a meal, sometimes after church and sometimes in the evening. There are tables and tables full of food, but many times the food is all desserts while other meals include turkey, chicken, beef, potatoes and vegetables. In these dreams, the church people quickly fill their plates, leaving no food for the visitors and people we do not know. Often we gorge ourselves on sweets until we are sick. This type of dream filled many nights over a short period. Each time I woke up, I felt sick to my stomach from all the rich food.

APPLICATION OR MEANING

As a church, we were taking in food (The Word, Hebrews 5:12) but not properly serving, or ministering, to the people of the community. We were so self-centered on learning and growing we seemed to be omitting the command to make disciples. We had mission outreaches and community outreaches, but our hearts were not pure. Much of this work resulted in making us feel good. It became a feel good club with our own congregation reaping personal self-righteousness for our own benefit. We could brag about how much work we did, but we were not even aware of how little the intended recipients were receiving.

Any church can fall into this behavior. We get busy with our ministry and our group, forgetting about the call to reach the lost and to make disciples. Pray and seek God about His ministry direction for your church. We do not want to become an introverted church, where all we care about are the current members or how much we do. We have to be aware of God's direction and calling for the church, and if we measure our results, we want to see good fruit from our efforts.

CONCLUSION

"Now there are diversities of gifts, but the same Spirit. And there are differences of administrations, but the same Lord. And there are diversities of operations, but it is the same God which worketh all in all" (1 Corinthians 12:4-6)

I n Acts 2, The Holy Spirit came to earth in a mighty show of power. Peter said the young men would see visions and the old men would dream dreams. The Holy Spirit administrates these activities. If we are open to what God is doing, we can all have a part in His ministry. This ministry includes reaching the lost and letting God use us to minister to each other as brothers and sisters in Christ. There are many gifts, but it is the same Holy Spirit. There are many administrations of the same gifts, but it is still the same Holy Spirit. Seek God as to what you are experiencing or would like to experience. Let the Holy Spirit lead and you will find an exciting and fruitful time of ministry for your life.

Many people have asked me to interpret their dreams. I do not always have an immediate interpretation, and sometimes the dreams are so personal that God does not show me the meaning. Some people are disappointed when I share with them that their dream seems not to be from God. Others are scared when they receive the meaning. God is not a mean God. If the dream seems scary, it may be because we are out of fellowship with Him or we are on a wrong path. However, God is not trying to hurt us. He loves us. The gifts He gives us are for the body so we can edify each other and grow in the fullness of Him.

My prayer is that people learn to discern and hear God's voice themselves. We learn what God's voice sounds like by studying His Word, The Bible. Jesus said his sheep know His voice. However, without spending time in His Word and getting to know how He speaks, a person does not know how to identify His voice. When a person repents and gives their life to Jesus, God gives them the ability to recognize His voice. However, the enemy is also watching and ready to talk to you. If you do not continue in the study of His Word, the enemy will speak to you and could lead you astray. Learning to hear the voice of God requires a time of growing and understanding.

I continue to dream and have visions. This book is only a small compilation of dreams over my lifetime. I will be publishing more of these visions and dreams in book two entitled Heavenly Experiences. Look for it in the spring of 2016.

MINISTRY TO YOUR GROUP

F aye and I have the anointing to minister spiritual gifts, including words of knowledge, words of wisdom, healings, prophecy, etc. We would welcome the opportunity to minister to your group or your church. Our mission is to bring people to a closer walk with Jesus and to impart spiritual gifts to others through the laying on of hands. No group is too big or too small.

Faye and Carlis contact information:

Carlis Stuber Ministries
PO Box 20623
Bloomington MN 55420
or
7107 S Yale Ave #113
Tulsa OK 74136-6308

Carlis 612-387-6310
Faye 612-387-6311
www.carlisstuber.com
brothercarlis@gmail.com

SHARING FOR A REASON

I wrote this series of books to call attention to God, not me. These books are to encourage others to seek God for Divine Revelation and to offer true-life experiences for those who may be skeptical about how God is working in and through them. Almighty God is not a casual spectator in our lives and this world's affairs. Rather, He is actively involved in the lives of individuals. Jesus stated, *"I will never leave you nor forsake you" (Hebrews 13:5)*

He has not left us nor forsaken us. He is working a good work in us until the day of completion. Part of that process is God interacting with His children through the process of dreams and visions, just as He said would happen. *"And it shall come to pass in the last days, saith God, I will pour out of my Spirit upon all flesh: and your sons and your daughters shall prophesy, and your young men shall see visions, and your old men shall dream dreams"* *(Acts 2:17)*

My prayer, as you read these books, is for you to seek God regarding dreams and visions that you might be having. A prophet once told me: if you are having dreams, and you do not know what they mean, then ask God. He is more than willing to give you the interpretation. Asking is very accurate advice. Perhaps you are a person who has never experienced dreams or visions. When Peter spoke the words of The Holy Spirit in Acts 2, there were no qualifications given for dreams and visions except this: Your old men will dream dreams, and your young men will see visions. All men, women, and children are included.

I spent years seeking God for an answer to the question, why was I having dreams both as a child and a young man. God revealed this to me; the statement regarding young and old is not about physical age but is rather about spiritual age. My sights, even as a very young person, were set on things above. I sought God through prayer, His Word, and meditation. My meditation consisted of walking for hours through the fields and woods of our family farm, as I prayed earnestly for answers to the many questions I had regarding who God was and why we are here. God answered me through dreams, confirmations of dreams, interpretations of dreams and signs, both on earth and in the heavens. I am still receiving confirmations from dreams I had as a young boy.

Every person, every life, has a purpose. The Bible states that some items (people and gifts) are for everyday use while others are for special occasions. Our responsibility is to seek God to determine our gifts and our callings in this life.

Using our gifts and talents, it is our responsibility to work and fulfill the tasks that God assigns us. Using our gifts and callings does not mean that we will be serving in full-time ministry. Some are called to be doctors, some lawyers, some machinists, some housekeepers, some politicians, some preachers, some teachers, etc. We all have callings and gifts.

I was called, "from the womb," to help reach a lost world for Christ. Called from the womb means God had chosen me before I was born to serve Him in ministry. One of the gifts God has given me and developed in me since I was little is dreaming and interpretation of dreams. Like everything we do, there is a learning time. Some of my earliest dreams were kind of silly, as I look back on them, but I was not yet mature enough to handle the larger issues for which God was preparing me. As you read these books, you will gain an understanding of how God uses people to speak to others, even to nations. God is showing me in dreams things that are yet to happen. Some of the dreams are about scary events. Other dreams are about extremely pleasant events. As I grow in the Lord, He can trust me with greater wisdom and knowledge of Him. The book of Proverbs declares, "If we are diligent in our business, we will stand before kings, and not in the presence of mean men." If we use our gifts diligently, then we will have an opportunity to deal with good people, perhaps even kings.

With this gifting of dreams and visions also has come a gift of interpretation of dreams. Many people have asked me to interpret a dream they are repeatedly experiencing. They know there must be a reason for the dream but do not understand what it means. Some of these people are not born-again and do not have the understanding of how God works or do not have a renewed spirit to interpret the dream. Many times God will use a dream or vision to get someone's attention to lead that person to Himself or a greater understanding of Him.

APPLICATION OR MEANING

As you read these pages and stories, I encourage you to seek God about any dreams you are having. If you are not having dreams, then ask God for them. There were no qualifications set in Acts 2. The verse states that God's Spirit would be poured out on ALL men.

God desires to be an active part of our lives. We need to take the time to sit quietly and listen to His voice. We should also be ready to journal or record what we think God has spoken to us in dreams or other ways. By journaling, we create a contextual and accurate record of the words. God loves you. Listen to Him and He will speak to you.

ABOUT THE AUTHOR

I believe it is important for the reader to have a little background about me. I could hardly expect the reader to accept or believe all these stories without some knowledge of who wrote these things. Here is a short glimpse into my life.

I grew up on a dairy farm in Wisconsin. Some people would say that we were isolated there in the country. We had a small farm of about 240 acres, including about 40 acres of woods. Across the road from us was a two square mile block of mostly woods and a few other farms. As a child, I would go into these woods and preach to the trees. I was a fan of Billy Graham, and I watched and studied him from the time I was nine years old. About 30-40 Holstein cows also enjoyed my preaching while I was growing up.

Our family consisted of Grandma, Mom & Dad, five girls, and four boys. When I was young, it was easy for me to relate to the Bible stories of Joseph and David since I am the seventh of nine children. I think it had to do with being the younger son. I also had this stirring in my spirit that I was set apart as they were; a stirring I started to understand better when I was about nine years old.

At the age of nine, I felt God calling me to preach, so I started preaching to the trees and cattle. I never dreamed at that age that anyone would be interested in what I had to say. In our culture, children were to be seen and not heard. We learned that young and carried it throughout adulthood. Some of us are learning late in life that God will use us to speak to others. Is that you? If so, please begin to speak up.

I suppose some might say I was a strange kid, maybe somewhat different from others. I was bashful and shy and did feel different. Some might have called me a silly heart or day-dreamer if they knew what I was thinking. Maybe some people did. One person stated he always saw me as a dreamer. One of my favorite activities as a child, even into my teen years, was to walk the fields and dream about what the world would be like if there were no sin. I would sit on the hillsides at night and watch the lights of the television towers in the city visible only from the top of the hills. I would watch them for hours pondering how God would use me to reach out to others. Some might call this awkward or weird. I call it spending time in God's school of understanding. I would never tell anyone about the dreams I was having. I did not want ridicule for them. In retrospect, I believe God prompted me not to share these dreams. By not sharing these dreams, God used them to build me into a strong and mature person, made in His image and not in the image of any man.

Now I don't want you to get the impression that I was a geeky, goofy, introverted kid. Actually, I was a cute little boy who knew how to work a crowd to get attention. You might say I was even a little spoiled. I was a very blessed child. Having many older siblings often brought me added attention, especially from my older sisters.

When I was fifteen, we moved into a small town where my dad worked. Since my earliest memories, Dad always worked away from the farm leaving most, if not all, the chores up to the family. Mom and Dad worked very hard. Feeding, clothing and caring for nine children could not have been easy, but I do not remember ever being concerned about whether we would have food to eat or a place to live. For us, it was normal to have Mom home when the school bus stopped and let us off after school. My life brought little or no outrageous drama, great sadness, intense pain, or uncertainty, but rather it was a peaceful time. I was happy and at the same time sad. Somehow, I felt so different from other people.

From my earliest remembrances, I thought this was normal. Even though I received plenty of attention, inside of me was a lonely, sad feeling, which I never shared. After all, didn't everyone see or experience the same type of events? Then as I entered my school years, I quickly learned that not everyone saw life in this same way. Making friends outside of the home was exciting and fun. There were always the usual boyhood competitions about who had the biggest Dad, who had the best dog that ran the fastest or who was the strongest. Through all this, I never stopped wondering or seeking who God was and what He was doing with me.

Over the years, I have had many experiences with God. I have been to heaven twice, maybe three times. Like Paul, I do not know if it was in the body or out of the body. When I was nineteen, I had an experience with God that forever changed my life. It was not during a time of intense worship or even while in church but happened while I was driving my car. I remember exactly where I was and can still see the circumstances surrounding this experience. I was meditating on salvation, and how a person can know for sure they will go to heaven. In fact, I was seeking God fervently. I wanted to know how I could be sure, that I was going to heaven when I died. The church told me, I had to be baptized and take communion. Every time I took communion, I knew I would ultimately sin again. Between communion Sundays I feared I would sin, then maybe die, and miss heaven.

As I rounded a curve in the highway, the words came into my spirit as if someone grabbed me and shoved them into me. The words were: You have to believe, but not just believe you have to BELIEVE. The emphasis on BELIEVE was so overpowering that I could scarcely drive any longer. This event sent me on a search to find out what it meant to believe. Shortly after that, I had the opportunity to hear Billy Graham in person. His message stirred my spirit, and I suddenly found myself standing in front of him, repenting of my sin and accepting Jesus as my Savior. This involved BELIEVING, or trusting, that Jesus death and resurrection was sufficient for all time to erase my sins and add my name in the Book of Life.

This event caused a renewing of the call of God to be in my life. Once again, I set out on a journey to learn how I was to serve Him. The only ministry I knew was pastoring because that is what I saw throughout my life. I spent years seeking how to fulfill this calling. However, there never seemed to be a place or distinct purpose for me in the ministry. Eventually, I gave up. The loss of this dream caused me to go into a deep depression. Through therapy and medication, I found my way out of this pit and, once again, I was on a journey to find God's purpose in my life.

TEN YEARS LATER

My life changed significantly in the next ten years. I now have a wife and two children, and, once again, I am backslidden. We lived in a small town, what some would call a bedroom community, about forty miles outside of Minneapolis, MN. Our house was new, and the neighborhood was mostly young families with children the same age as our children. They played together, rode the school bus together, and shared houses for playtime. Life seemed reasonably stable and good, but in my spirit was a restlessness I could not seem to shake off.

I had a good job working in the corporate office of a Fortune 500 company. In this job, I shared an office with two men who loved God. One day as I walked into the office, I felt a presence so strong that it literally drove me to my knees. These men came over and explained the plan of God's salvation to me, and once again, I found myself repenting and seeking

God. I went home and shared with Faye that I was going to attend a David Wilkerson Crusade in Minneapolis. She also wanted to go, so we got a sitter and went to the crusade. I made the statement, "This is my last time. Either I truly meet God face to face, or I am going my own way." Well, I had an experience with God that left no doubt that He was real and that He was active in my life. We gave our hearts to the Lord that night and never turned back from Him.

I still had this burning to serve God. The dreams started coming almost every night. Faye and I sought God fervently. After moving several times, attending Bible school, and becoming ordained (Faye as a chaplain and me as a pastor and chaplain) we are serving God as best as we know how. Through all the experiences, there never seemed to be a place where I felt comfortable enough to say, " I am right where God wants me to be."

As we grew and served God, we often struggled with our finances. There were many times when I was laid-off due to cutbacks, businesses closing, or businesses being sold and moved. When the last company I worked for closed, I decided to teach manufacturing technicians a course on calibration. I wrote a technical manual, which I use in my classes, and I developed a website as best I could and put it on the Internet. Within six months, I started getting calls for training. I have continued to travel and present workshops for over sixteen years. I knew from the start that God was using this as a training ground for my next season of work.

That new season is the books God is showing me to write. I am sharing these dreams and visions for the benefit of the reader. Each dream and vision has an application applied to it because that is how God directed me to share these dreams.

I have prayed for each you who are reading these books and ask that you pray for Faye and me as well. I do not own these dreams. They are messages from God. Some are personal, and some are not. I have dedicated my life to serving others and helping others grow closer to God. This dedication will sometimes cause others to ridicule me, and others to embrace me. I give my life as a testimony to you and Jesus. By His grace, I will fulfill all He has for me to give to you.

Rev Carlis Stuber

CPSIA information can be obtained at www.ICGtesting.com
Printed in the USA
LVOW11s0855181215

467125LV00001B/1/P

9 781498 456890